How to Save Money Even If You're Broke!

Financial Common Sense

JW Warr

ISBN 13: 978-0-615-51644-8

Cover design by MamiSerwaa, 3ps Graphical Solutions
Cover art by Margaret M. Stewart, Shutterstock.com

CONTENTS

Foreword

Most of you have experienced what is commonly called "Training by Fire Hose" where the training staff provides an enormous amount of information in an amazingly short time, and you walk away feeling overwhelmed. Well, that very adequately describes my first experience in front of JW Warr. In just 30 short minutes he set in motion a sequence of events within me that has caused a fairly dramatic change in my life; all for the better. This book is not training by fire hose, but I can assure you that as you work your way through it, you will encounter many revelations that might just change your life for the better as well.

Extracted herein is the accumulation of 30 years of experience and the creative genius of JW Warr, who has only a high school diploma, but the equivalent of a PhD in the REAL world! JW has endured the continual "ups and downs" associated with building and owning businesses, has endured the trauma of bankruptcy, has built an insurance and securities business from scratch and achieved the highest ranking possible in the profession, and more recently has initiated a new business in the owner-financed mortgage industry.

The ever curious JW continually studies the industry to try to find a way to create capabilities that benefit the client. I am gratified that I was able to assist in the early efforts that led to the creation of this book and in assisting with the book as well. JW is a creative genius. I am a more pragmatic 'show me' kind of person. JW would throw ideas and concepts at me and I would attempt to validate them. Over time and through constant changes I developed model after model as he continually challenged me with his 'WHATIFs'. We established a relationship where we fed off of each other in our developmental efforts, and the end result was a totally new way of assisting clients with new financial capabilities that benefited them instead of the industry.

This book accomplishes two specific goals. It teaches the reader the basic fallacies of conventional wisdom and the basics of how to use common sense to analyze finances, but it also teaches the reader to 'think outside of the box,' which is the basic premise of JW's companies. Furthermore, it employs JW's mannerisms, both in speech and in constructive thinking. Throughout you will read and experience what we call 'JWisms.' These are embedded on purpose – both because they provide anecdotal insight as to what is being said or taught, but also because JW said to leave them in!! He makes no pretense about being better or more knowledgeable than anybody, and in fact, prefers to be just a "good ol' boy" that happens to know a fair amount about the finance arena, and wants to share that knowledge.

So ... I present to you a collection of JWisms and a wealth of financial insight. Read. Enjoy. Test. Question. Second Guess. Refute. Whatever. If you learn something new ... great! If you began to question your current financial situation ... even greater! That is the goal of this book. Think outside the box. Question everything. Ask multiple sources. Learn, and keep learning. You are your best ally, but you can also be your own worst enemy. Galileo said, "You cannot teach a man anything; you can only help him find it within himself."

-- Jim Beall

Preface

Too Many People Specialize in the Possible
Way Too Many People Specialize in the Just Passable

Norman F. Dacey, a renowned financial writer, once said, "Where, now will the American people find a champion willing and able to harness the strength of this financial giant? Who will lay the present sorry mess open to the light of day? Where will we find a man with the temerity to face these latter-day "untouchable," to stand in the path of this juggernaut and cry "Halt?" When he is found and takes the job and does it, he will never be forgotten, for he will have brought the American people more financial independence and self-respect than a hundred years of Social Security."

I believe this was written about Art Williams; if it wasn't, it should have been. If ever I had a Hero it would be Art. Art Williams grabbed one of the most powerful industries in the world by the collar and shook it. He used common sense to attack the deceit in the life insurance industry. He took his little part-time ragtag army of A.L. Williams's agents to war against cash value life insurance. His battle cry was "I want Pru" (Prudential). Within a very short time A.L. Williams became the national leader in selling life insurance and sure enough, beat Prudential. Because of the example of Art Williams I know what I am going to do is possible. I believe that as more and more people learn how money really works, the fingers that the financial industry has around our throats will lose their grip and we will regain control of our own destinies. So, let's see if we can't get ahold of their collars and start to shake.

I think Jack Handey, a writer for Saturday Night Live, put his finger on the problem in one of his Deep Thoughts, "It's easy to sit there and say you'd like to have more money. And I guess that's what I like about it. It's easy. Just sitting there, rocking back and forth, wanting that money."

Land of Opportunity

The things that keep us poor are few in number and can be easily fixed. What you are about to learn is that many times "Conventional Wisdom" is a poor substitute for "Common Sense." I'm not just going to show that to you, I'm going to kick down the conventional wisdom door.

My real work, as I see it, is to help you see the world as it is and show you how to make it bow down to your wishes, a world where no one can steal your future with bad investment advice, deceptive lending practices or bad tax advice.

This is a journey to Truth. A journey of a thousand miles begins with one step. It starts with one person, then spreads block by block, city by city, state by state, there will be no way to stop it, and it's been my personal experience that a great effort will be put forth to stop what I am about to teach you from reaching the masses.

This then is a "Declaration of War."

I know this sounds overly dramatic but when I turn on the light of common sense truth, the conventional wisdom cockroaches will first scatter then attack as if their lives depended on it.

If people can regain their reason to hope, and those who have given up a "reason" to believe to believe again, if we can inspire an army to come together, we can turn the page on debt. We could end this thing that has kept us poor, kept us stressed and destroyed our futures. We could write a new chapter in the American Story.

I've been told my dream of changing the financial future of America was naïve. I was told the American people would never be able to listen because the Financial Giants would never let them hear even a small bit of the truth. That a little bitty company like Financial Blueprinting was too small to make a difference. The person that said that has obviously never tried to sleep in the same room with a mosquito. I remember what George Washington said before the Battle of Lexington, "I have lost every battle and failed every attempt; if I have to do this by myself, by God I will."

New friends have started joining now and believing we can change the world. Because of them, we can now stand in front of this Goliath debt and make it tremble.

In the weeks to come, we need you to do your part. You can become a crusader for hope and an agent of change. How can little old you become a crusader? To become a crusader just forward this to three people.

These are solutions that many will call 'too good to be true' or 'pie in the sky.' They are indeed good and true but it's not a 'pie in the sky;' when you see your friends become able to pay off all their debt, including their mortgage, in five years. It's not too good to be true when you can afford to send your kids to private school. It's not a pipe dream when you see someone that you introduced to us retire at 65 and with the ability to afford the lifestyle always dreamed of.

Once you become aware of the facts you cannot ignore them. It would be like trying to ignore a rhinoceros in your kitchen. Most of your dreams about your future were buried alive as youth or was dragged from you by the years. The good news is they are still alive; you have to but dig them up and dust them off. Yes, they can still serve you well. Imagine suddenly you will have something to look forward to.

You will learn how other people have recovered and prospered in these economic times.

If you don't understand the tax system, if you just file the simplest tax return, if you have debt and a job, we will teach you how to turn every dollar of your current debt into many dollars at your retirement. I know what I am getting ready to say sounds crazy, but I will give you proof that it's true. Are you ready for something that will blow your mind? Here it is; the more you are paying on debt the more money you will have when you retire. In olden times there was a science called Alchemy (a medieval chemical philosophy having as its asserted aim the transmutation of base metals into gold). I will show you how to change debt into gold—literally. Now I have to prove it!

▪ Fear Stops Everything Good and Preconceived Notions Lead Us Into Dark Places

We fear the math of finance like a child fears the monster under the bed, but there is no more a reason to fear the math than the monster under the bed. Let us simply turn on the lights and dissolve the monsters.

When my daughter Julie was at the University of Texas she was studying how to stop the spread of fire ants. The scientists thought that the answer might be to find the ant's natural enemy - a small fly that lays her eggs in the back of the fire ant's head and when the eggs hatch the fly larva feed on the ant and kill it. Everyone knows that ants are not afraid of anything – an ant will attack a fire, and it will sting an elephant. The scientists discovered that the fly only kills about 3% of the ants so it was hard to understand how the flies could control the spread of fire ants.

After studying the ants and flies the scientist finally discovered the secret. Any time a fly laid her eggs on an ant's head, the other ants would come over to the egghead to see what happened and when they felt the presence of the fly, they would hide. If a chicken tried to lay an egg in the back of my head, I'd hide too. When the flies are around, the ants are either checking out the victims or hiding. Thus, they are not gathering food. The shortage of food controls the ant population, but what causes the shortage of food is fear. The flies kill only 3% – the rest starved because they are afraid. Fear of contradicting conventional wisdom can cause you to starve also.

▪ It's Not Your Fault if You Have Financial Cancer

If you are struggling with your money, it's not your fault. Financial experts, ads, books, society, movies, and even your parents and friends are programming you with conventional wisdom to stay poor.

They aren't doing it on purpose. They aren't evil. They were simply programed with a conventional wisdom virus and are passing the virus to you, hidden in their everyday conversation or presentations. I will try to remove this virus from your system.

I've seen a lot of things that I don't understand, my phone bill, two-headed sheep and Rap music, but common sense is pure and simple. I've always been a country western guy in a rock and roll world. I don't think intellect should overpower wisdom, and I don't feel analysis should impede action. I try to keep things simple in a complex world. It doesn't matter what world you're in; common sense is the same. Everyone needs to increase their cash flow so everything I do for my clients is oriented around increasing cash flow by using a simple easy to understand system.

▪ It's Good to Know What You Don't Know

It's good to know what you know ... and to know what you don't know. I think the most dangerous thing is to think you know what you don't know and that's where conventional wisdom hides. This is an example of the failure of conventional wisdom. Most of you can ride a bicycle, right? If you're riding down a street and you want to turn right, you simply pull the right handle bar toward you and the bike turns right, right? **Wrong!!** To turn right you push briefly on the right handle bar, which causes the bike to lean to the right and it turns. Even though you can ride a bike it works the opposite of how you think. Somehow your body knows how to steer, even if your brain doesn't.

Many of you may doubt what I just said about the way you ride a bicycle. You might just call a bicycle shop and ask them how to steer a bike. You could go on the internet and look it up or buy a book to see if you could learn how to steer a bicycle. I'm sure that people who sell bicycles know how they steer. If it's on the internet, well it must be right. If someone actually wrote a book on how to steer a bicycle, they have too little to do and probably have a second income.

If I were you, I would simply go ride a bicycle. Put your finger tips on the ends of the bars and go down a gentle slope (so you don't have to pedal) and push briefly on the right bar. If the wheel being forced to turn left does not cause the bike (and you) to lean to the right and subsequently cause a turn to the right, then stop reading this book because the laws of physics do not apply to you. If I'm wrong about this, I could be wrong about everything. If you don't believe me and don't test it yourself, you will not like the rest of this book. I am willing to prove everything I show you, and if you will not test the things I say, a chicken will probably lay an egg in the back of your head. You can sit in your Lazy Boy and push and lean all you want but unless you get on a bike and test my theories you will never get it. If you think the things I'm telling you in this book don't sound right, just get out the calculator and prove me wrong. Here is my email address JW@FinancialBlueprinting.com.

Unfortunately, your body has no natural instincts when it comes to math. If you've forgotten your multiplication tables ... if you never "got" algebra or (heaven forbid) calculus ... if you understand that 2 plus 2 does equal 4 (except in advertising and politics) ... if you can learn to punch the right buttons on a calculator... YOU CAN DO THE MATH!

I went to a breakfast meeting and sat next to the president of a large national bank in Albuquerque. He asked me what I did, and I told him I had a new way to do mortgages where I help people find the money to pay the mortgage off early and reduce the cost. He looked down his nose at me, pointed his manicured finger like a gun at my head and in a snobbish voice told me, and I quote, "We don't **believe** in pre-paying loans at our bank because then people lose the tax advantage of a mortgage." I told him, and I quote, "Pre-paying a loan is a financial tool, not religion; your **beliefs** are not based in facts." He told me that the average family was not financial sophisticated enough or disciplined enough to make decisions about what they needed – that someone had to make those kinds of decisions for them. Well, Bull! I just don't believe that! I believe that financial companies have gone to great extremes to complicate a simple business. To quote Ernest Hemingway, "My aim is to put down on paper what I see and what I feel in the best and simplest way." The financial industry's aim is to put so many words on so much paper that nobody can understand what it all means and feels stupid for their lack of understanding.

My experience has shown me that planning and investing in your future is simply a mathematical problem like 2 + 2 = 4, and a math problem has only one right answer. If you want to take control of your own finances all you need is good information, and you can make good decisions—it doesn't take a genius to figure this out. All you need is a map to reach your destination. Throughout this book, I will try to stick to the fundamentals. People spend their whole lives looking for a better way to "get rich quick" only to find out that if they had just gathered a few facts, done the fundamental little things and used common sense, they could be financially secure. With my TIDES System, you learn how to reduce what you pay in taxes, insurance, and debt and use the freed up money to pay off not only your debt but your mortgage in a very short time without affecting your cash flow.

▪ What's So Bad About Conventional Wisdom?

Heck JW, I'd listen to you, but you do not even have a bunch of letters after your name like CLU, CFP or PhD. Many breakthroughs in science come from outside the system. Experts are most thoroughly familiar with the already developed knowledge within the boundary of their field, but frequently, new discoveries come from 'outside'. Pasteur was not a MD. The Wright brothers were bicycle mechanics. Einstein was not a physicist but a mathematician, and Reagan was an actor. Myself, I have a PhD (public high school degree). All my knowledge comes from an understanding of the future value of money and my contempt for the conventional wisdom, and the biased teachings of vendors. Luckily my lack of a formal education has left me with "Uncluttered Thought."

Dr. Bob Froehlich in his book Where The Money Is says that today all finances are connected. The impact of what appears to be a somewhat minor, isolated event may eventually have a major impact on your retirement. He's right! Something as small as a $50 mistake each month for 30 years is catastrophic. I think Benjamin Franklin said, "If you watch your pennies – your dollars will take care of themselves."

When Dr. Bob autographed his book for me he wrote, "May you always know where the money is." Well, everyone, it's ten o'clock do you know where your money is? Remember it's the things you think you know (but that you don't know) that cause the most trouble. Let us go on a great adventure together "outside the box of conventional wisdom." Stop doing things that you don't understand just because a lot of other people do it that way. Just because all the dogs are barking up a tree doesn't make it's the right tree.

There was always a palace guard stationed in the middle of Red Square in Moscow during the 1900s. One day a new officer asked, why, even in the dead of winter, he had to assign a guard to stand in the middle of Red Square guarding nothing? After some research, the reason was discovered. Twenty years earlier one of the princesses was crossing Red Square on a sunny summer day and saw a beautiful flower growing between the cracks in the stone. She did not want anyone to step on the flower, so she assigned a guard to watch over it. She forgot about the flower and the guard shortly thereafter, and no one asked "why" for 20 years ... that bare spot was guarded 24 hours a day, 7 days a week!

I feel that we have been guarding a bare spot in the financial industry for over a hundred years. The flower died many years ago, so it's time you ask the question, "Why does everyone guard an idea that died years ago?" Today's economy does not resemble the economy of 5 years ago, much less 50 years ago, so we need new ways to deal with it.

I believe, as does Dr. Froehlich, we have a responsibility to teach our kids how money works, to give them the tools to build a life that is debt-free and full of promise and to know that today all finances are connected and what affects our friends and neighbors affects us. The things I am about to show you are guarded secrets. It's no fun knowing a guarded secret if you can't tell someone, so tell your kids at least.

▪ THE LAND OF OPPORTUNITY

We are going to set the country on a course to fulfill its promises as "The Land of Opportunity."

Too many people just have faith that their finances will work out and they will by some miracle end up on top. They don't seem to realize that the only thing that floats to the top is a dead fish. There is a special name for these people—they are called "The Poor." You on the other hand are doing something that less than 1% of the population will do; you are educating yourself. My good friend Peggy Cook says that she never has made a bad decision with the information she had at the time, but she reserves the right to change her decision if she gets better information. First of all, allow me to congratulate you on your decision to take control of your financial future! This will make you feel better than you have felt in years.

If you are poor when you retire, even a real good excuse won't help your financial condition of "you're poor." We all realize that Social Security will not be there for most of us when we retire, and we have to do something more than just blindly investing in the stock market and 'hope' for a good return. I was in a Pack 'n Sack the other day and I met a man in line in front of me. His name was Buck and he was a plumber. He asked what I did for a living and I told him I showed people how to save money even when they were broke and retire when and how they want. I show people a way to do that without changing their cash flow. He was next so he told the clerk to give him $10 worth of lottery tickets. I think that after what I told him he was embarrassed because he turned to me and said, "I buy $10 worth a day; it's my Redneck Retirement Plan." Those words were a lot more embarrassing than they were funny. Needless to say Buck will not be reading this book.

▪ Taking Control

Taking control of your retirement accounts now is the first step to achieving peace of mind and financial security for when you can't work anymore. Because of my unwillingness to grow up, my mother told me something that is stuck in my brain. She said, "You may not be young forever." Too many people have what I call "Scratch-off Retirement Plans;" every few years they scratch-off another square hoping for a windfall. Every time their 401k or IRA loses money they just hope it will recover. They base their retirement plans on faith that everything will be alright. You must always remember that faith is a religious concept, but it's not a very good retirement plan. Time and high returns are your friends when you are young, but even high returns can't help you when you've run out of time. The market dropped a few years ago and it has been inching up, ever so slowly since. It's been said that "if you don't sell when the market is down you haven't lost any money," but in truth you have lost money and more importantly, you've lost time. You can always get more money....

I forget the kid's name in The Karate Kid, but before Mr. Miyagi would teach him karate he made him paint the fence, sand the deck and wax the car. (You know, wax on-wax off.) The kid was impatient to learn karate and thought Mr. Miyagi was tricking him into doing free labor. Mr. Miyagi then demonstrated that "paint the fence, sand the deck, and wax on-wax off" were the basics of karate, and that indeed the hours of what seemed to be busy work were in fact the basic training for all lessons to come. I told you that story so you will understand that I am going to simplify and explain a new system for first finding the money in your current financial situation and then making your money grow (wax on-wax off). I will show you how you can benefit no matter what your financial situation is, without giving up your current life style or affecting your cash flow. When was the last time you felt fantastic about your financial future? Remember how you felt financially the day you got your allowance as a kid? Well it's time to feel that way again.

Time to Find the MONEY

▪ How to Get a Financial Blueprint for Your Financial Future

Connventional Wisdom tells you that finances are too complicated for your uneducated mind. You need an expert to tell you what to do and when to do it. Never mind that you don't understand how the things you are giving your money to work, the financial expert will guide you to prosperaty. They will put your money in things you don't understand and charge you fees that you can't figure out and charge you a commission for doing it all. But don't worry I have enlarged the fine print below "Sign here", ("Past performance is no indication of future performance and there is a chance that you could lose your principal.").

Sign here X________________

Past performance is no indication of future performance and there is a chance that you could lose your principal.

Why do we ever sign things like that?

In the fable "The Emperor's New Clothes," two scoundrels who had heard of the Emperor's vanity decided to take advantage of it.

"We are two very good tailors and after many years of research we have invented an extraordinary method to weave a cloth so light and fine that it looks invisible. As a matter of fact it is invisible to anyone who is too stupid and incompetent to appreciate its quality."

I am going to look at taxes, insurance, debt essentials and savings like the child, who had no important job and could only see things as his common sense eyes showed them to him, the child who said, "The Emperor is naked."

Common Sense is screaming at you.

My preacher once told me the story of the time he was driving across Lake Ponchetrain on the 27 mile bridge with his wife and newborn daughter. He saw a car sitting in the middle of the road and a man waving his arms. It crossed the preachers mind that this was an attempt to stop and rob him, and he did not want to endanger his new family. He decided to go around the stranger and not take the risk. As he approached, the stranger realized that Pat was not going to stop. The stranger jumped in front of the oncoming car to stop it. When Pat screeched to a stop he realized why the stranger had risked his life to stop him; a barge had hit the bridge and caused it to collapse, if he had driven another ten feet everything Pat loved would have been belted into that sinking car.

I sometimes feel like the stranger. I am standing in front of a collapsed bridge waving my arms franticly trying to warn everyone of the danger ahead. I'm sure it never crossed Pat's mind that the bridge he had crossed so many times before was not safe. What I am trying to warn everyone about is the danger of conventional wisdom. You may think "danger" is to strong a word, but if you will just stop and look at the math you, will see for yourself why I call your old paradigm of thinking dangerous.

Nobody will ever tell you the truth, everybody only tells you what is politically correct and restates the conventional wisdom like "over 85% of the people who work here contribute to our 401k," and "mutual funds let you dollar cost average into the market."(Reduce voilitility by depositing the same amount each month.) Don't forget one of my favorites, "If you don't sell in a down market you didn't lose any money." We have been lulled into a place of comfort where we let the "experts" make all the hard decisions for us. In this time in American history there are totally new financial problems that the average families are facing, we need totally new solutions. We need a new paradigm.

Albert Einstein, when ask why he gave the same final exam every year, responded, "The questions are the same, but the answers have changed." Since these are new problems, there needs to be new solutions. What I am about to say will have financial experts wanting to have me "burned at the stake." I will be hated for my willingness to dare say that the Emperor has no clothes. I can't sit still and watch what is called "conventional wisdom" totally replace "common sense." Carl Sagan said, "We simply accepted what the most widely available and accessible source of information claimed is true. For our naiveté we are systematically misled and **bamboozled**."

I know what I am about to tell you sounds crazy, but I beg you to think about it before you decide. If you have what I call a "Whoo moment" where my thought process hits you like a bucket of cold water, your stinking thinking is over and you can now start fixing your future and saving for retirement—even if you're broke, let me say those words again **even if you're broke**. Here it is; don't forget all the things financial experts have told you, in fact try to remember it all and see if all of their conventional wisdom can stand up to these common sense solutions.

You don't need to have a lot of letters after your name like CPA, CLU or even PhD to understand finances, you only need some good information and some good old common sense. The experts will always try to make you feel inadequent so you won't use your own common sense and will rely on their slick presentation instead.

▪ LOST IN THE DEBT WOODS WITHOUT A FINANCIAL COMPASS

Why do so many people spend so much in their lives not knowing where they are and moving in the opposite direction from where they want to be? I'm not talking about geography, I'm talking about financially. We know what we want. **What we want is generally the things that get us in debt**. We need to learn how to get the things we want without debt. If we can get the things we want without acquiring debt it would be like getting a 50% discount. A 50% discount on all the things we want would be a dream come true. Too much debt eventually stops us from acquiring the new things we want. I don't want to belabor the point but if you can get a 50% discount on the things you want because you have no debt you can have more of the things you want. All poverty is caused by choice—too many of the wrong ones. Nobody makes bad decisions on purpose; they make the best decision they can with the information they have at the time. The secret to making good decisions is having good information. The trouble with getting good information is it's hard to find and it's very hard to tell the difference.

I will send a short, easy to fill out form that you can email to me at jw@financialblueprinting.com or fax to 512-628-6303 and I will send you back your own personalized Financial Blueprint. I will give you a financial tool that you would have to spend thousands on, for free. Go to (http://screencast.com/t/eaPnijraE) for a tutorial of what a Financial Blueprint looks like.

▪ FINANCIAL BLUEPRINT

You wouldn't build a house without a plan or a blueprint, yet most people never plan for their financial future. You know the feeling you have that "I know I need to get started saving for my retirement but..." I'm guilty of it myself. Then one day an insurance salesman you know from your softball team tells you he can show you a plan. You didn't know what to do in the first place, so if you can get someone else to design your financial future that would be great. After all you know him and he makes his living in finance. So you turn the planning for your future over to someone else. Do you know how much time someone else will spend on thinking what will be best for you and your family? **NOT MUCH!** Do you know what someone else has planned for you? **NOT MUCH!** How much of the plan was aimed at you and your wants and needs? **NOT MUCH!** You just take it on faith that this expert will design a plan that you can start and never think of again until that great day you retire to a life of luxury. Financial plans are not like a religion; religion works off of faith, a financial plan should work off math.

A Financial Blueprint is not a speculation or hope, it's **MATH**, it's 2+2=4. The Financial Blueprint is a simple plug your numbers in and hit ENTER. Your plan will appear.

You need to begin with the end in mind. In other words, you need to know what you want and when you want it. I don't like to ask people "What's your goal." Too often we are forced to come up with some "goal" answer by a teacher or a boss or even a team member on the spot. We always make up something that will be accepted by the leader, not nessaceraly what we want. I believe we all know what we want. So what do you want when you retire?

Getting a retirement plan is not like buying a house. When I was younger and would go looking for a house to buy, I never thought of what it would look like. I knew that when I saw the right house I would know it when I saw it. Sure enough, that statagy always seem to work out. Now you can't do that if you are going to build a house. You can't just go out and buy some bricks and lumber and start building. You need a blueprint. There are no used or previously owned retirement plans for sale out there. The only way you can have a retirement plan when you retire is if you built it yourself. The only way it will be done right is if you do it yourself, so you need some easy to follow instructions on how to design a retirement plan.

A Financial Blueprint is the best way for you to get a clear view of where you are financially. It will give you easy to follow directions on how to fund the lifestyle **you want** and retire the way **you want** when **you want**. The purpose of a Financial Blueprint is to *find the money* to fund your retirement—from your debt. This program was not designed for the wealthy, it was designed for the average American to find the wasted money. Because most of us accept the common explanation of finance, we do not truly understand we are continually bamboozled.

I was talking to a group of ladies after one of my seminars and I was trying to tell them that I help people reposition their assets but what I said was, "I help people repossess their assets." The more I thought about that misstatement the more sense it made. The Financial Blueprint will reveal to you how to **REPOSSESS** your assets from the IRS, the gigantic insurance industry and the greedy mortgage establishment. Once you are again in control of your money and understand how to make it work for you, you can start making your own financial decisions.

This free Financial Blueprint will not only put you on the road to financial independence, it will have you definatly shaking your fist at the financial giants that have conspired against you.

The things you need to build a solid financial future are

1) A dependable place to put your money where it pays a high fixed interest and backs your money with real collateral (Owner

Financed Mortgages).

2) A system to get you **completely out of debt** (Financial Blueprint).
3) A little time to get it done.

What Do You Want?

I'm sure the first thing you want in your retirement plan is that it has to be easy to do because we all know the easiest thing to **<u>not</u>** do is a retirement plan. So this plan cannot require you eat rice and beans for the next 25 years. This plan needs to be workable and flexible. Retirement that isn't backed up by a good plan can be longer than a Yoko Ono solo and twice as annoying.

In the Blueprint example they want to retire in 20 years. Combined they make $4,500 per month.

		Joint Income
No. of years to retirement:	**20.0**	**$4,500**

They have a fixed 6 percent 30 year mortgage that started at $150,000 with a payment of $899.33 per month and they have lived in the house for 7 years. Last year they got a $3,200 tax refund.

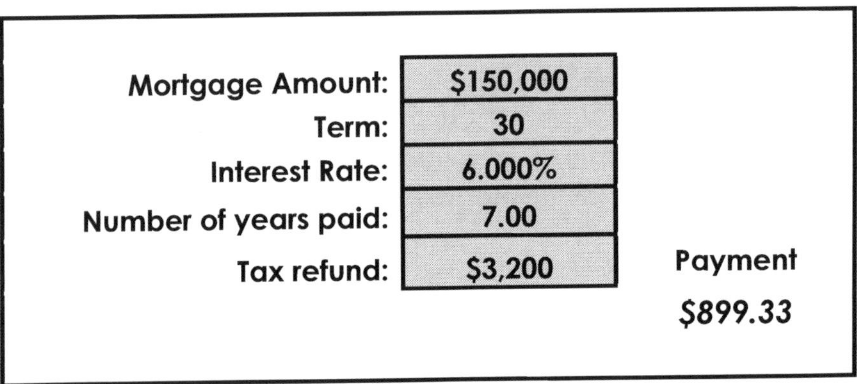

Mortgage Amount:	**$150,000**	
Term:	**30**	
Interest Rate:	**6.000%**	
Number of years paid:	**7.00**	
Tax refund:	**$3,200**	**Payment**
		$899.33

The first thing to know is what do you want and when do you want it? If you want to retire in 20 years, then that is how long you have to build up your savings. Let's say you are retiring tomorrow and your house was paid for and your kids have moved out for the second and last time what do you want to do?

..........Since I'm not there to ask you the questions let's pretend OK?

Let's say you want to travel. Now you can't stop there; nobody wants to just travel all the time, they want to go somewhere special, somewhere they have always wanted to go. If you would like to go to Paris for example, do you want to stay at the Paris Motel 6 or at the Four Seasons? Do you want a individualy wrapped Genieva chocolate on your pillow every night when you get back from eating at a fine resturant or do you want a room with linoleum floors? Do you want to spend a week seeing the real Paris or do you want to spend 1 of your 3 days in Paris on a tourist bus? Well, because you did a retirement plan and worked the plan every month you can go to an ATM anywhere in the world and withdraw from you retirement savings. How much do you want to withdraw in today's dollars?

This is a little mathmatical trick I think you should know. If your answer is $3,000 per month then multiply $3,000 X 172 = $516,000. That means that when you retire you need to have saved $516,000 because if you invested $516,000 at 7 percent, it would pay you about $3,000 per month forever. This works with any monthly amount. You now know what you are aiming at for retirement and when you need it. The Financial Blueprint will now gather some more information and help you find the money to reach your goal.

There is an 18% penalty on tax refunds!

The first money to go after is the easiest; tax refund:
http://www.irs.gov/pub/irs-pdf/p15.pdf

Using the IRS's own instructions if you make $1,600 every 2 weeks and you got a $3,200 tax refund you are over paying your taxes. A $3,200 refund ÷ 26 pay periords = $123 per pay periord or $266.67 per month. If you look at your pay stub and see that they are withholding $163 per check and now you know you are paying $123 to much then subtract $123 from $163 = $40. Look at the chart and see how close you can get to $40. Change the withholding allowances to 6.

MARRIED Persons—**BIWEEKLY** Payroll Period
(For Wages Paid through December 2011)

And the wages are–		And the number of withholding allowances claimed is—										
At least	But less than	0	1	2	3	4	5	6	7	8	9	10
		The amount of income tax to be withheld is—										
$1,500	**$1,520**	$148	$127	$106	$84	$64	$49	$35	$21	$7	$0	$0
1,520	**1,540**	151	130	109	87	66	51	37	23	9	0	0
1,540	**1,560**	154	133	112	90	69	53	39	25	11	0	0
1,560	**1,580**	157	136	115	93	72	55	41	27	13	0	0
1,580	**1,600**	160	139	118	96	75	57	43	29	15	1	0
1,600	**1,620**	163	142	121	99	78	59	45	31	17	3	0

Now we need to look at their debt.

DEBT (List in <u>ascending</u> order by <u>amount owed</u>):

	Owed	Monthly Payment
Visa	**$1,750**	**$90**
Chase	**$1,800**	**$95**
Bank of America	**$3,800**	**$210**
Student Loan	**$7,000**	**$392**
Car Loan	**$16,000**	**$489**
DEBT TOTAL :	***$30,350***	***$1,276***

They owe $30,350 in credit cards, student loans and a car loan. They pay $1,276 per month.

They have $28,000 in an old 401k they rolled over.

IRA and 401k Rollover:$28,000.00

They can take the $266.67 we freed up from the refund every month and put $200 per month in their IRA and the other $66.67 can go toward getting out of debt.

Money Currently Available for Debt Payoff: $67

They take the freed up $66.67 and add it to the $90 they were already paying on the Visa Card and now pay $156.67. It takes 13 months to pay off. This is the beginning of one of the best feelings they ever will have; that "out of debt feeling." Once the $156.67 is freed up, it is applied to the Chase bill. They have been paying the minimun payment on all the other bills. So instead of paying $95 to

Chase they now pay $251.67 and it takes 4 months to pay off Chase. Now this is getting big, they have paid off Visa and Chase and now have $251.67 to add to Bank of America. You can see how fast this works. In 26 months they are debt free except for their mortgage. I feel like I should write this with a lot of fanfare instead of in such a matter of fact way. Debt free in 26 months and it didn't change their cash flow.

Remember they did not effect their cash flow. They are still living on the same amount of money each month that they were before we met.

Total amount available per month to apply towards debt payoff:		$66.67	
	Owed	*Monthly Payment*	
	$1,750	$90.00	
	13 month	***$156.67***	
Funds available to retire debt =		$156.67	
	Owed	*Monthly Payment*	
	$1,800	$95.00	
	4 months	***$251.67***	
Funds available to retire debt =		$251.67	
	Owed	*Monthly Payment*	
	$3,800	$210.00	
	2 months	***$461.67***	
Funds available to retire debt =		$461.67	
	Owed	*Monthly Payment*	
	$7,000	$392.00	
	0 months	***$853.67***	
Funds available to retire debt =		$853.67	
	Owed	*Monthly Payment*	
	$16,000	$489.00	
	7 months	***$1,342.67***	
Total number of payments to retire all debt:		26	months
Or		2.17	years

Mortgage

Now they needed to look at the biggest debt they have; the infamous fixed rate mortgage. I will explain what a rip-off mortgages are later, but for now let's look at how to pay that puppy off.

They paid off all their debt in 26 months and now have $1,342.67 per month that they were paying to debt that now they can use to pay off their house. They add the $1,342.67 to the $899.43 and now pay $2,242 per month on their house.

JW's Optimization Technique

Interest	Principal	Ending Balance	First
750.00	149.33	149,850.67	**Month**
Cumulative Interest	**Cumulative Principal**	**Ending Balance**	**Payment**
Cumulative Interest	**Cumulative Principal**	**Ending Balance**	**Payment**
8,949.89	1,842.02	148,157.98	899.33
17,786.17	3,797.65	146,202.35	899.33
26,501.83	5,873.89	144,126.11	899.33
35,089.44	8,078.20	141,921.80	899.33
43,541.08	10,418.46	139,581.54	899.33
51,848.39	12,903.07	137,096.93	899.33
60,002.45	***15,540.92***	***134,459.08***	899.33
67,993.81	18,341.47	131,658.53	899.33
75,812.44	21,314.75	128,685.25	899.33
83,141.52	38,204.28	111,795.72	2,242.00
89,284.50	58,965.24	91,034.76	2,242.00
94,147.00	81,006.69	68,993.31	2,242.00
97,650.03	104,407.62	45,592.38	2,242.00
99,709.73	129,251.86	20,748.14	2,242.00
100,048.16	150,000.00	**Paid Off**	

They started their Financial Blueprint in the 7th year in shaded area above. They continued to pay $899.33 payments for the next 26 months then when the debt was paid they added the freed up money and paid $2,242. Their house was paid off in 5 more years.

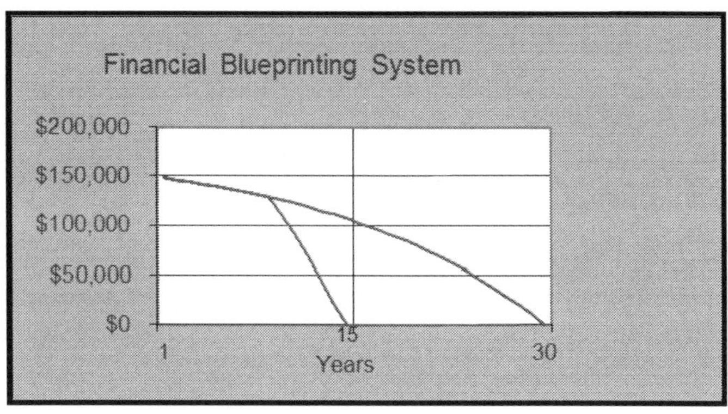

The long line old way; short line new way.

Time to pay off all debt:	7 years and 10 months
Now invest full amount of:	$2,242.00 in a retirement account at 9% for 12.17 years.*
Potential growth for retirement account:	$890,976 at 7% for 12.17 years.
Potential growth for retirement account:	$812,705

They wanted to retire in 20 years and had $28,000 in their old 401k and they freed up $267.67 in taxes of which $200 went to savings at 9%. By the time they retired they would have **$890,976.**

Next is a copy of a Financial Blueprint. If you would like one they are free. Email me at jw@FinancialBlueprinting.com and I will send you the form.

*Real Estate Note

Contact Information
www.FinancialBlueprinting.com
info@FinancialBlueprinting.com

		Joint Income
No. of years to retirement:	20.0	$4,500

Mortgage Amount:	$150,000	
Term:	30	
Interest Rate:	6.000%	
Number of years paid:	7.00	
Tax refund:	$3,200	Payment $899.33

	Owed	Monthly Payment
Visa	$1,750	$90
Chase	$1,800	$95
Bank of America	$3,800	$210
Student Loan	$7,000	$392
Car Loan	$16,000	$489
DEBT TOTAL :	*$30,350*	*$1,276*

IRA and 401k Rollover / Freed up from taxes	$28,000.00	$200.00

"FOUND" MONEY & HOME BASED BUSINESS CONTRIBUTION:

Money Currently Available for Debt Payoff: $67

Financial Blueprinting debt stack strategy, debt is paid off in **26 months**

Time to pay off all debt: 7 years and 10 months

Now invest full amount of: $ 2,242.00 in a retirement account.
At 9% for 12.17 years.

Potential growth for retirement account: $890,976

This is for illustration purposes only based on the information provided. Actual numbers will differ.

EXAMPLE:

Mortgage	**$ 150,000**
Interest Rate	**6.00%**
Payment Principal & Interest	**$ 899.33**

	Regular Mortgage				**JW's Optimization Technique**			
First	Interest	Principal	Balance	Cost I-P	Interest	Principal	Balance	First
Month	750.00	149.33	149,850.67	***$5.02***	750.00	149.33	149,850.67	Month

Yr. #	Cumulative Interest	Cumulative Principal	Ending Balance	Cost Int. to Prin.	Cumulative Interest	Cumulative Principal	Ending Balance	Payment
1	8,949.89	1,842.02	148,157.98	$4.86	8,949.89	1,842.02	148,157.98	899.33
2	17,786.17	3,797.65	146,202.35	$4.68	17,786.17	3,797.65	146,202.35	899.33
3	26,501.83	5,873.89	144,126.11	$4.51	26,501.83	5,873.89	144,126.11	899.33
4	35,089.44	8,078.20	141,921.80	$4.34	35,089.44	8,078.20	141,921.80	899.33
5	43,541.08	10,418.46	139,581.54	***$4.18***	43,541.08	10,418.46	139,581.54	899.33
6	51,848.39	12,903.07	137,096.93	$4.02	51,848.39	12,903.07	137,096.93	899.33
7	60,002.45	15,540.92	134,459.08	$3.86	***60,002.45***	***15,540.92***	***134,459.08***	899.33
8	67,993.81	18,341.47	131,658.53	$3.71	67,993.81	18,341.47	131,658.53	899.33
9	75,812.44	21,314.75	128,685.25	$3.56	75,812.44	21,314.75	128,685.25	899.33
10	83,447.68	24,471.41	125,528.59	$3.41	83,141.52	38,204.28	111,795.72	2,242.00
11	90,888.23	27,822.77	122,177.23	$3.27	89,284.50	58,965.24	91,034.76	2,242.00
12	98,122.07	31,380.84	118,619.16	$3.13	94,147.00	81,006.69	68,993.31	2,242.00
13	105,136.47	35,158.36	114,841.64	$2.99	97,650.03	104,407.62	45,592.38	2,242.00
14	111,917.87	39,168.87	110,831.13	$2.86	99,709.73	129,251.86	20,748.14	2,242.00
15	118,451.91	43,426.73	106,573.27	$2.73	**100,048.16**	150,000.00	**Paid Off**	
16	124,723.33	47,947.22	102,052.78	$2.60				
17	130,715.95	52,746.51	97,253.49	$2.48				
18	136,412.55	57,841.82	92,158.18	$2.36				
19	141,794.88	63,251.40	86,748.60	$2.24				
20	146,843.57	68,994.62	81,005.38	$2.13				
21	151,538.02	75,092.08	74,907.92	$2.02				
22	155,856.40	81,565.61	68,434.39	$1.91				
23	159,775.50	88,438.41	61,561.59	$1.81				
24	163,270.71	95,735.12	54,264.88	$1.71				
25	166,315.87	103,481.87	46,518.13	$1.61				
26	168,883.22	111,706.42	38,293.58	$1.51				
27	170,943.31	120,438.25	29,561.75	$1.42				
28	172,464.83	129,708.63	20,291.37	$1.33				
29	173,414.58	139,550.79	10,449.21	$1.24				
30	173,757.28	150,000.00	0.00	$1.16				
	173,757.28	**150,000**	**TOTALS**	**116%**	**100,259.56**	**150,000**	**Paid OFF**	

Financial Blueprinting System

$200,000
$150,000
$100,000
$50,000
$0
1
15
30
Years

Loan Paid Off ==> EARLY!!

This is for illustration purposes only based on the info. provided. Actual figures will differ depending on the lender and charges a lender may apply. Please refer to your contract or lender for prepayment policies which may affect these calculations.

This illustration, and any benefit of acceleration shown, assumes all payments are made via transfer from your checking account according to the loan and the payment schedule you select. This is for illustration purposes only; actual savings may vary.

CURRENT DEBT OVERVIEW	Owed	Monthly Payment
Visa	$1,750	$90.00
Chase	$1,800	$95.00
Bank of America	$3,800	$210.00
Student Loan	$7,000	$392.00
Car Loan	$16,000	$489.00
	$0	$0.00
	$0	$0.00
Totals	$30,350	$1,276.00

Total amount available per month to apply towards debt payoff:	$66.67

Owed	*Monthly Payment*
$1,750	$90.00
13 month	***$156.67***

Funds available to retire debt =	$156.67

Owed	*Monthly Payment*
$1,800	$95.00
4 months	***$251.67***

Funds available to retire debt =	$251.67

Owed	*Monthly Payment*
$3,800	$210.00
2 months	***$461.67***

Funds available to retire debt =	$461.67

Owed	*Monthly Payment*
$7,000	$392.00
0 months	***$853.67***

Funds available to retire debt =	$853.67

Owed	*Monthly Payment*
$16,000	$489.00
7 months	***$1,342.67***

Total number of payments to retire all debt:	**26**	months
Or	**2.17**	years

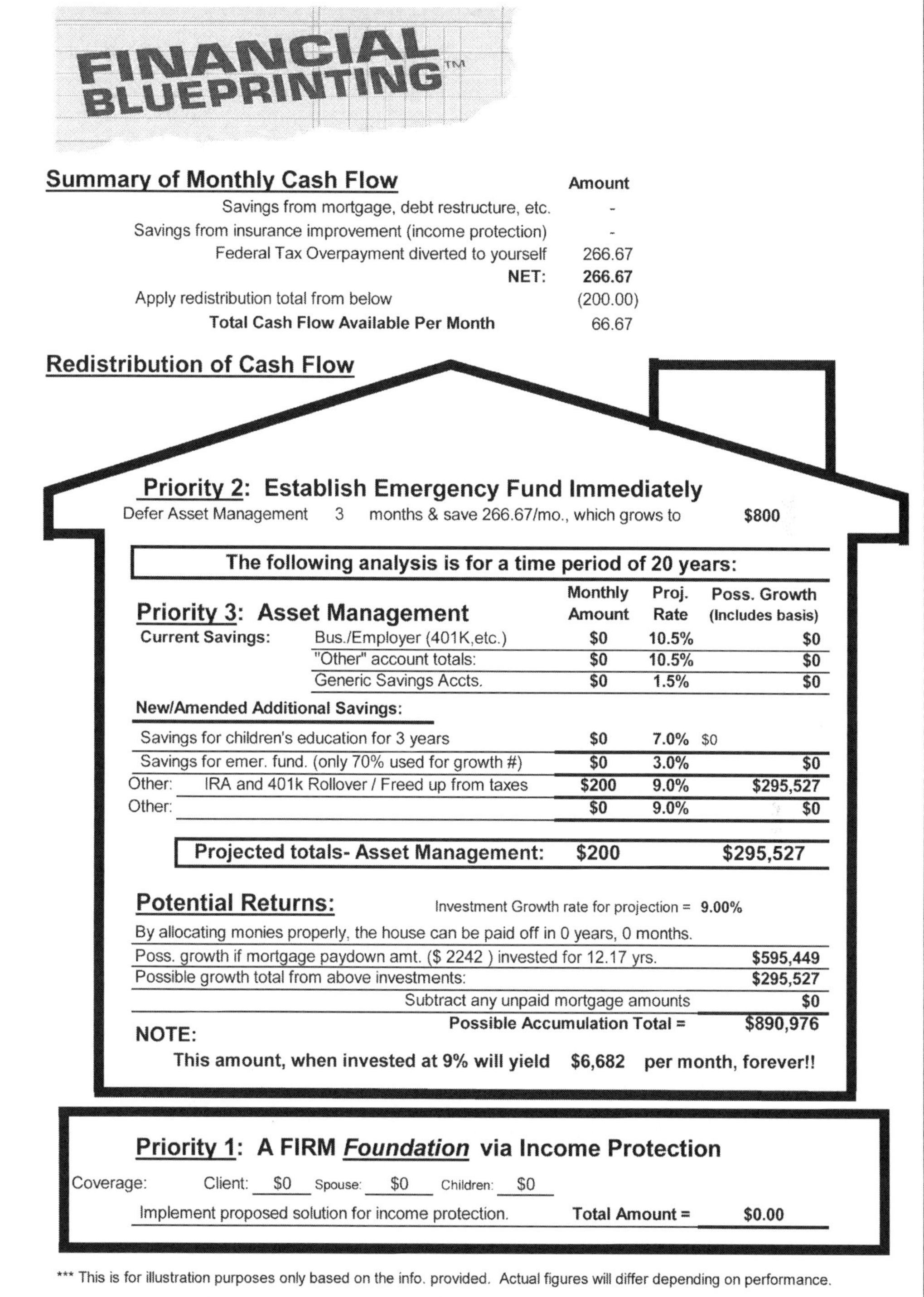

FINANCIAL BLUEPRINTING™

Summary of Monthly Cash Flow

	Amount
Savings from mortgage, debt restructure, etc.	-
Savings from insurance improvement (income protection)	-
Federal Tax Overpayment diverted to yourself	266.67
NET:	**266.67**
Apply redistribution total from below	(200.00)
Total Cash Flow Available Per Month	66.67

Redistribution of Cash Flow

Priority 2: Establish Emergency Fund Immediately

Defer Asset Management 3 months & save 266.67/mo., which grows to **$800**

The following analysis is for a time period of 20 years:

Priority 3: Asset Management		Monthly Amount	Proj. Rate	Poss. Growth (Includes basis)
Current Savings:	Bus./Employer (401K,etc.)	$0	10.5%	$0
	"Other" account totals:	$0	10.5%	$0
	Generic Savings Accts.	$0	1.5%	$0
New/Amended Additional Savings:				
Savings for children's education for 3 years		$0	7.0%	$0
Savings for emer. fund. (only 70% used for growth #)		$0	3.0%	$0
Other:	IRA and 401k Rollover / Freed up from taxes	$200	9.0%	$295,527
Other:		$0	9.0%	$0
Projected totals- Asset Management:		**$200**		**$295,527**

Potential Returns: Investment Growth rate for projection = **9.00%**

By allocating monies properly, the house can be paid off in 0 years, 0 months.

Poss. growth if mortgage paydown amt. ($ 2242) invested for 12.17 yrs.	$595,449
Possible growth total from above investments:	$295,527
Subtract any unpaid mortgage amounts	$0
Possible Accumulation Total =	$890,976

NOTE:

This amount, when invested at 9% will yield $6,682 per month, forever!!

Priority 1: A FIRM *Foundation* via Income Protection

Coverage: Client: $0 Spouse: $0 Children: $0

Implement proposed solution for income protection. **Total Amount = $0.00**

*** This is for illustration purposes only based on the info. provided. Actual figures will differ depending on performance.

Fill out the Data Input Form for your free Financial Bluebrint. Email to jw@FinancialBlueprinting.com

JW Warr

Retirement Data Input Form

When do you want to retire? How many years from now? ___________

If you were to retire tomorrow with all your debts paid, how much money would you like each month?
$___________

	You	**Spouse**
If you have a plan with a previous employer, approx. how much is in that plan?	$_______	$_______
If you have an individual IRA, approximately how much is in that plan?	$_______	$_______
Other assets available at retirement? (Stocks, Bonds, CD's, Mutual Funds)	$_______	$_______
Does your current employer have a plan available?	☐ yes ☐ no	☐ yes ☐ no
How much do you have in your 401K or retirement plan through work now?	$_______	$_______
Does your employer contribute? _______ If yes, how much?	______%	______%

	First Name	MI	Last Name	Birth Date	Age
CLIENT				__/__/____	_____
SPOUSE				__/__/____	_____

ADDRESS: ____________________________________ Home Phone _______________

CITY: ______________________ State _____ Zip ________ Work Phone _______________

Do you normally receive an income tax refund? ☐ yes ☐ no

How much did you get last year? $________

Do you anticipate receiving a refund this year? ☐ yes ☐ no

If yes, how much to you anticipate? $________

I need to see a copy of a recent pay stub to see what you pay in federal income taxes.

Do you have an emergency fund? ☐ yes ☐ no

If yes, what is the current balance? $ __________

Are you purchasing your home? ☐ yes ☐ no

If yes, I also need to know when your mortgage started.

After this information is entered into the computer, I'll recommend which strategy is best for you -- either debt stacking or a debt restructuring.

	Debts	Current Balance	Minimum Payment	Actual Payment	Interest Rate
Mortgage start / /	$________	$________	$________	$________	________%
______________	$________	$________	$________	$________	________%
______________	$________	$________	$________	$________	________%
______________	$________	$________	$________	$________	________%
______________	$________	$________	$________	$________	________%
______________	$________	$________	$________	$________	________%
______________	$________	$________	$________	$________	________%

How the TIDES System Works

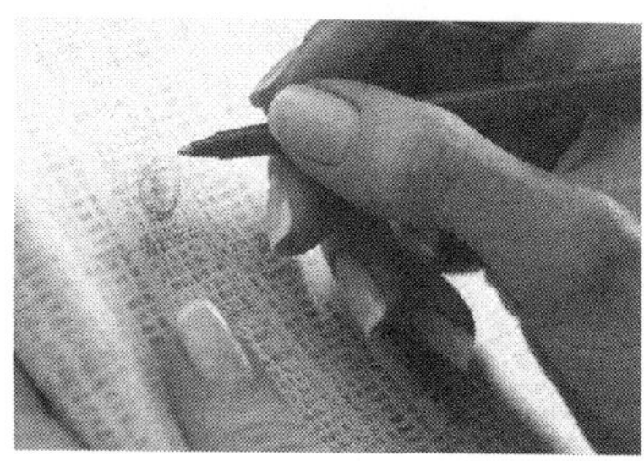

The main problem people have with saving money is they are broke at the end of each month. How can you save any money if you are broke? No matter how smart your investment advisor is, it makes no difference if you don't have any money to invest.

My dad once told me that he had lost $50,000 in the cattle 'bidness' (Texas for business) that day; he said that the price of cattle went up and he didn't have a damn one. I believe that is the major problem with financial experts; they tell you where to PUT your money not where to FIND it.

I will give you first a system called TIDES which will enable you to lower your **T**axes, reduce the cost of most of your **I**nsurances (life, health, home owner, renter's and auto) and then free up money to pay off all your **D**ebt. Once you are debt free you will have a lot more money for the **E**ssentials (food, gas, cloths, education for your kids, etc.). You will also have enough to **S**ave for your retirement. I will give you a blueprint to build financial independence (Financial Blueprint). Nobody builds a house without a blueprint.

I was at the theatre the other day where I read a sign about the rating system for movies; like G, PG, PG-13, and R. The sign said something that I think fits finance like a glove; "**For the system to work you must understand the system**."

How can we trust our families' future and life savings to a system that we not only don't understand, but the experts refuse to explain to us?

You already know that you have to invest in your financial future. You want to invest in an easy to understand system while earning a return, interest rate, or at least a couple of points above inflation. Unfortunately, no one has provided you with the steps to wealth creation. As such, few Americans are taking actions that really lead towards retirement saving.

CNN announced in the summer of 2010 that 43% of all Americans had less than $10,000 in retirement savings. The following are some more alarming statistics about our savings habits in this country:

- 56% of workers between the ages of 25 and 34 have less than $10,000 in savings, as do the 46% between ages 35-44, 38% between 45-54, and a **mind boggling** 29% of workers over age 55 have less than ten thousand dollars in their retirement savings.

If this is you and you know you need to start saving but you don't know how or where you will find the money, you're lucky because you have already done the hardest part, you started reading and learning. I'll show you what to do and where to find the money.

- Only 51% of all Americans even have a retirement program
- Only 40% of people under 35 years old have a retirement account and most will use their account up before retirement

How did this happen? Debt is the answer. Back in the 1980's, Americans saved $10.00 out of every hundred earned. Nowadays, most Americans are lucky to save $1.00 out of every hundred in fact because of our debt most of us spend $110 out of every $100 we earn. We are making more; we are just not keeping more—in fact we are not keeping any.

This is an Important Paragraph.

I believe that most people would rather save money in places where they are forced to spend it instead of where they want to spend it. Would you rather cut back on the money you spend on your family or the money you spend on taxes, insurance and debt? That's kind of a no brainer isn't it? This premise is the basis for how we find the money in your current budget to get you out of debt and into financial independence.

43% of all American have less than $10,000 in retirement savings.

Today's essentials, such as health insurance, car insurance, medical expenses, gas, etc… are unavoidable. In addition, people are paying higher taxes than they need to. These days, people are spending a larger percentage of their income on debt than at any other time in history.

People aren't educated on how to save money. In fact, we are told how to sacrifice the things we want in order to free up a few pennies for our future. Forbes, Money and other financial magazines always tell people where to save money. They always tell you to put your money in the same old "Conventional Wisdom" places that got you in trouble in the first place. In fact Forbes recently published a stupid survey stating that teens who were educated on how to set financial goals, how to save money "properly," and provided with financial options (all conventional wisdom) were over 150% more likely to save for the future than those who didn't have the knowledge. The article didn't state how many were able to save enough money to retire with a good life style; they only said they were more likely to save. 93% of all statistics are made up; including that one. I think they made up the survey to help them sell their conventional wisdom products. Never think that all those magazines give you the information because you need it; they do everything they do to sell ads to the very same people they are recommending. There's that good old common sense again.

There aren't many incentives to save. CD rates, money market accounts, savings accounts, Treasury Bills, etc... are all paying under 2% and don't appear to be increasing anytime soon. The stock market is volatile and people are reluctant to invest, fearing a double dip recession. Even if you have money left over at the end of the month, where do you put it for peace of mind retirement planning? It's hard to make up for the commissions you pay when you buy gold, stocks or mutual funds. So what do you do?

Read on, my friend!

Understanding how to save for your financial future isn't a magic trick, nor does it require a special gene that you were either born with or without, rather it is a skill set that anyone and everyone can learn. It's a fact that if you reduce your taxes and pay off all your debt you will have more money for your retirement. One might say its applied common sense. This book is dedicated to discussing creative ways on how to create more cash flow for you without altering your lifestyle.

I call it the TIDES and it goes as follows:

- ***T****axes.* Find simple, legal ways to reduce your taxes and you will increase your cash flow.
- ***I****nsurance.* Look at your current life insurance policy. If you are investing in cash value life insurance (like 70% of Americans), you can easily free up some money for your retirement. Plus there are ways to make most of your insurances like life, home owners, health and auto at least partly tax deductible because they can all become business expenses.
- ***D****ebt.* I will detail a simple strategy to allow you to get out of debt successfully without having to go on a 'rice and beans' diet. I will give you the tools to accomplish this goal.
- ***E****ssentials.* Once you have straightened out your debt, you will find you have more money for the essentials in life, like food, cloths, education, transportation and retirement.
- ***S****avings.* Finally, once you have everything taken care of; create your own retirement savings account so you will have a comfortable nest egg for yourself in your golden years. I have told you the type of investments I believe work best.

I think you'll find my process very simple to understand and execute.

Again, when the American people are educated and put their minds to it, they can accomplish any goal they set. If you have better information you make better decisions. So let's get educated, develop a painless plan, and build your future!

A Simple Plan

If you could reduce or eliminate what you are paying in taxes and use that money to pay off debt and use the combined, freed up money to pay off your house in about 7 years, you could then design your financial future without changing your cash flow. This is what a Financial Blueprint does for you. If you can work this simple system you can save money, even if you are broke.

▪ How Taxes Really Work

In 1913, almost all of the Congressmen were wealthy businessmen. At the time the only income the federal government collected was from tariffs, duties and fees that were paid by the businesses. The wealthy business-owning Congressmen decided that they would rather the average wage earner pay for the federal government instead of them so they told the average wage earner that we needed an income tax.

They told us that it would really be a tax on the rich because (we must have been very naive back then; taxing the rich is like trying to nail Jello to a tree) the average wage earner had a lot of kids and they could write them off, and because they were good charitable people they could write off charitable contributions, and because the rich had a lot of money that they wanted to lend to the average citizen they would let us write off the interest we paid them. This might have been the start of our current debt society because no matter what interest rate they charged you could simply write it off your income taxes. The business owners would only write off their expenses (which turned out to be almost everything.) We bought their story and passed a constitutional amendment to start an income tax. What were we thinking?

At the end of each year we were supposed to send in whatever tax we owed but the system didn't seem to work very well. During WW II, the government had to sell War Bonds to raise money to pay for the war so some diabolical genius came up with a cunning plan that the IRS could raise more money if the income tax was taken out before the wage earner got his check. Boy, were they right; revenues went up 1000%. Since most of the men were off to war and became accustomed to not making much money and having the government do everything for them, when they got back they just accepted that the tax was withheld before they got their check.

The average American overpays income taxes resutling in something called a 'tax refund' by over $2,400 a year. The IRS doesn't pay you interest on this money.

The IRS made the instructions for figuring the correct amount to withhold so complicated and the threat of an IRS audit so scary that the average American overpays income taxes resulting in something called a 'tax refund' by an average today of over $2,400 a year. The IRS doesn't even pay any interest on your voluntary overpayment.

IF YOU DON'T START A HOME-BASED BUSINESS, YOU DON"T UNDERSTAND THE MONEY SAVING BENEFITS!

The income tax was set up to punish the wage earners and reward the business owner. The well-kept secret is to be both a wage earner and business owner. Most people don't want to give up their secure job with its retirement plan and medical insurance. They know how to do their job but don't know how to be a business owner. They don't have the money or time to run their own business. We would all like to have our cake and eat it too, well being an employee and a business owner lets you do just that.

Let's look at the advantages to owning your own business. First, the income tax was designed to allow you to deduct business expenses, not personal expenses.

If you set up a computer and desk in your home and it takes up 10% of your square footage you can deduct 10% of your house payment, 10% of your home owners insurance and 10% of your utilities. If you use your car as part of your business you can deduct that percentage of your car payment, automobile insurance and repairs. You can hire your family and pay them to help with the business. As part of your family's compensation plan, you can pay all of their medical expenses which includes all the medical insurance you pay at work and any other medical expense like co-pays, glasses dental or over the counter drugs.

Remember that the tax laws were written to help the business owners. If you are making $5,000 per month at your regular job and start a home-based business you can now take advantage of the laws. If you own a home-based business, it is possible for you to reduce your taxes to about 15%. By reducing your taxes to 15% and your medical expenses to 15%, you have freed up a lot of money each month to quickly pay off your credit cards, automobiles, student loans and mortgage. You could eliminate all debt in just a few years without changing your lifestyle. Instead of the IRS keeping you poor, you can use your increased cash flow to make yourself rich. That is "the rich man's secret;" use the IRS or they will use you.

The way to accomplish this task is by starting a simple, part-time business with the motive being to make a profit. If you have a profit motive, then you will be able to take advantage of some of the beautiful tax write-offs that congress gives to business owners.

First step is to find a simple, low cost business that you can do part-time. Obviously, I'm not advocating you to quit your job and commit to a business nor am I suggesting you suddenly drop your life savings into opening a shop at a strip mall. I'm simply saying that you should find a passion and figure out a way to try to make some extra money with it. Whether you profit or not, you will still be able to take advantage of tax write offs.

Try an MLM company or product. They offer very low overhead costs, and with minimal, part-time effort, you should be able to generate some revenue. Again, the goal is not to make a million dollars (though it's okay if you do) but to create a business **to bring in revenue** and take advantage of some of the write-offs.

Once you figure out what your passion is, then make a company. You can start a Sole Propiatership or create an LLC, either one is inexpensive and not very time consuming. You can 'Google' your states secretary of state department to find out the forms needed to start a business. Generally speaking, you'll need to register a trade name and fill out articles of incorporation, which should be less than 6 pages of combined paperwork. After the state takes the fee to set up your LLC, then get an EIN number and open a business account and you're ready to roll. Go to:

https://sa2.www4.irs.gov/modiein/individual/legal-structure.jsp

Why is it important to be a business owner? When you are an employee, you are taxed on your labor before you pay yourself. When you are a business owner, you are able to pay expenses first, and then pay the government. Remember this is a part-time business; you still keep your full-time job and all the security and benefits it gives you.

Remember, the income tax was designed to allow you to deduct busines expenses, not personal expenses.

Let's take a look at a very simplified example of the difference between paying taxes first versus paying expenses first. We'll assume that both the employee and the one that owns a business but doesn't make any money yet. They both make $10,000 per month and both have the same expenses of $5,000 per month.

Employee vs. Business Owner/Employee

Monthly	Employee	Business Owner/Employee
Income	$ 10,000	$ 10,000
- Tax Deductible Expenses	0	($5,000)
= Total Taxable Income	$ 10,000	$ 5,000
- 30% Income Tax	($ 3,000)	($1,500)
= Net Income	$ 7,000	$ 8,500

In this simplified example, the business owner/employee will bring home over $1,500 more per month from his job than the employee without a part-time business by rearranging the order of how he is taxed! Remember, the business owner didn't make any money in his business. Do you see now why having a small business is so important? You may only save $300 per month but that's $3,600 per year or about $720 savings. How many car payments can you make with $720?

When you start a "home-based" or "part-time" business, it is most important that you satisfy the requirements of the tax rules by having a **strong profit motive**. If you have a strong profit motive, IRS will not be a problem. Don't worry about the "hobby" rule if you don't show a profit. The tax laws were written with the idea that it may take some passing of time before you start making a profit and profit is not mandatory, only a **strong profit motive** is. The important thing is that you **have a strong profit motive from the start** and the best way to show a strong profit motive for your home-based business is to be able to show money coming in from the business.

Don't mix your business money in the same account as your personal money. Get an EIN tax number (Financial Blueprinting will apply for you) and set up a business checking account. It's hard to prove a profit motive if you don't have any money coming through the business. Make sure you don't comingal your money with the business.

You are already spending most of your income on your children, home, medical expenses, vehicles and vacations. Wouldn't it be nice if you could convert some of those expenses to a tax deductible category, and **increase your monthly take home pay by several hundred dollars simply by setting up a home-based business?**

Of the 157 or so of congressionally mandated tax benefits for small and home-based businesses, there are **six benefits** that represent the greatest value for the effort. As you evaluate the following deductions, keep in mind that these six categories can result in tax write-offs (deductions) that will total in the thousands which can easily result in a **huge tax savings.**

▪ Here Are Some Of My Favorite Write-Offs

- MEDICAL EXPENSES: Home (and many small) business owners can deduct 100% of medical expenses. This includes **medical insurance premiums** (even if you are paying at you full time job), office visits and co-pays, dental, pharmaceuticals, glasses and other costs not covered by insurance. The secret here is to set up a business Medical Reimbursement Plan that allows your business to pick up the costs of all medical expenses for all of the employees of the Company. This benefit will average about $3,200 or more a year per family. Currently, only 1% of taxpayers eligible for this Medical Expense deduction are taking advantage of it! So hire your spouse and contract to pay all of him/her's spouse and children's medical expense.
- HIRE YOUR KIDS: Pay each of your kids (age 6 – 18) up to about $4,700 per year, to perform "meaningful" work for your home-based business. The entire amount is considered a business expense and there is no income tax or social

security taxes due for such payments. You can pay each of your children $4,700 a year and have them purchase their own clothes, toys, college, weddings, etc. It's your choice, AND, IT IS YOUR MONEY! Pay Uncle Sam, or pay your children – it's the same money! And, it is fully deductible as a home business expense! You can set up a checking account for your kids and put the money in every month. The IRS does not care where the kid's money is spent; the car payment or rent could be paid from this account.

- HOME OFFICE: A home business owner can write off any portion of the home that is dedicated and used exclusively for business as a business expense. The average amount of this deduction amounts to about $2,800 per year. Only 10% of taxpayers who could take this deduction are taking advantage of this major tax benefit.

No, this is not a red flag to the IRS to spur an Audit!

- BUSINESS VACATION TRIPS: If you plan your vacations properly, such trips can be combined with business trips so as to make many of the expenses involved tax deductible. Proper planning and documentation is required. This planning could easily save you hundreds of dollars in taxes. Next time you go on a vacation, put an ad in the paper for your destination, and conduct some business meetings while you are on vacation. Deduct most of the cost of this vacation as a business expense, even if part of your vacation is for recreation purposes.
- BUSINESS MILEAGE: IRS allows you to deduct 51 cents (the amount adjusts yearly) for each mile that is documented as having a business purpose. You can even convert commuting miles into business miles by performing business

tasks on your way to and from your regular day job. You should document all mileage with a mileage log in each of your vehicles. Not taking advantage of this strategy is like throwing money out of your window!

All of the above deductions are based on existing family expenses. <u>You don't have to change a thing to take advantage of these deductions other than start a home-based business.</u> Then, all you are doing is converting household expenses into tax deductible expenses with the effect of lowering your tax bill!

One of the best places to find money to pay your home off early is a home-base business. With enough legitimate write-offs you can reduce or eliminate you taxes from your full-time job. Then you can use the extra money to pay your house off early without hurting your cash flow. On a $100,000, 30 year mortgage at 6% if you applied $200 per month, you saved in taxes by owning a home-base business you could pay your house off in 16 years and 8 months, and save $58,452. You can send the money to the government or send the money to your retirement fund.

The Financial Blueprinting Example: On a $150,000, 30 year mortgage at 6%, if you applied $67 per month you saved in taxes by owning a home-base business, you could pay your house off in 7 years and 10 months, and save **$73,498** in interest payments.

I know the hardest thing about keeping records is keeping receipts. You need to move into the 21st century. I personally use ExpenseDocs.com to "Simplify Documentation." I take a picture of my odometer with my phone when I leave my house and when I return. Remember, it's currently 55.8 cents a mile. I also take a picture of my receipts in the restaurant and this application will send it to my computer. I actually enjoy keeping records. This is the solution to the trauma of tax time you have been searching for. Demo is available by contacting bill@expensedocs.com or calling 512-585-7108. It will save you thousands and it's only about $12 per month.

HOW LIFE INSURANCE REALLY WORKS

▪ THERE ARE TWO REASONS TO OWN LIFE INSURANCE

1) To replace your income if you die
2) To pay a life insurance agent the highest commission you can.

If you don't think #2 is a great reason to buy life insurance then just buy term life insurance. Never buy life insurance that has a return built into it (Universal, Variable Life) because the cost of insurance goes up inside the policy every year.

Conventional Wisdom tells you that you need life insurance so if you die your family can pay off the debt, replace the income, pay off the mortgage and educate the kids. This is one of those times when Conventional Wisdom and Common Sense are the same. However, the insurance industry is not happy just doing the right thing. There is not enough profit for them in just doing the right thing so they came up with a much more profitable plan for them by offering a return inside the insurance policy.

I just want to make this simple. I don't care if it offends anyone; life Insurance that promises a return is to be avoided.

After my father died my mom asked me to go through some of his stuff and see if I wanted anything? I found a jewelry box with a rather large diamond ring in it. I showed it to my mom and she said, "Oh you can have it, it's a cubic zirconia." She had a real I karate diamond so I held them up side by side. I was surprised but the cubic zirconia looked a little better than her real diamond.

About a month later I had a jeweler give me his universal cash value life insurance policy to review for him. When I brought the policy back to him I ask if he would mind looking at the ring I got from my father. He got out his little one eyed jeweler glass and then he held it up to his mouth and breathed on it, he then told me it was a cubic zirconia. I ask how he could tell. He said to put the stone to your mouth and breathe on it. If the stone stays "foggy" for 2-4 seconds, then it is not real. Real diamonds will have cleared by the time you look at them. I then said "so unless you know diamonds someone could sell you a cubic zirconia." I then pulled his cash value universal life insurance policy out of my brief case and said, "Someone sold you a cubic zirconia policy." It looks like a life insurance policy but the cost of insurance goes up every year and the only way to keep the policy in force is to borrow money from the cash value account to pay the premium. By the time he reached old age the increasing cost of the insurance depletes the cash value to 0 and the policy self-destructs. He needs to buy life insurance to protect his family and invest his money somewhere else. The only way to do that is with whole life or term.

I believe that when Americans are informed, we make the smartest decision. So let's inform you by breaking down what insurance is and what it's used for. I will describe how to use whole life and invest the cash value later.

The purpose of life insurance is simply "Income Protection." To be blunt, it is to replace your income when you die. This insurance is supposed to financially protect your family until you have your retirement account fully funded to take its place. This is called "The Theory of Decreasing Responsibility." If something happens to you, you want to make sure that your family can continue to live comfortably without you. *If* your retirement savings grow your need for life insurance shrinks. I don't like ***if***.

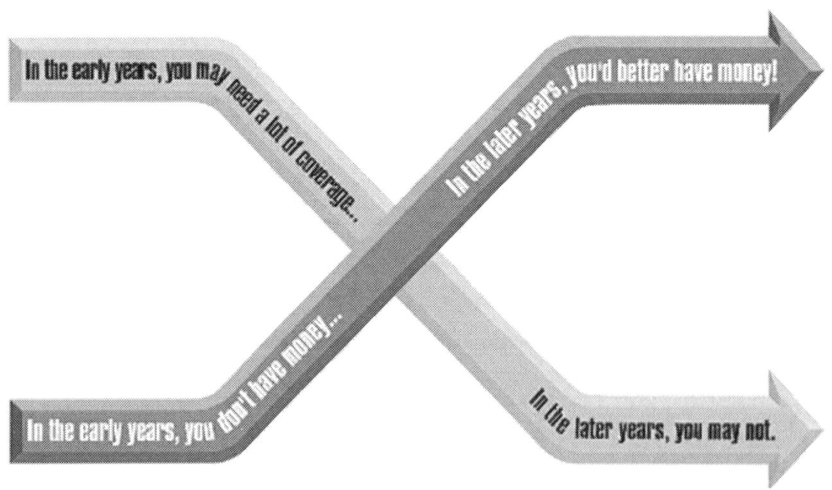

I've change the way I think lately about this simple theory; With the markets moving up and down so much I now believe that you also need to safe guard your retirement with an insurance policy that will last you whole life. If you are 50 years old or older you don't have as much time to build up that retirement savings.

Most people who are in their 20's or 30's have a house with a mortgage, They have a spouse, children, and other expenses as well, but what they probably don't have yet is a nest egg and if something happens, they want protection for their family. Isn't this the time you need life insurance the most?

Once you reach retirement age, hopefully you've created your nest egg, you're children have left the house, you've downsized your expenses, you are able live off your retirement funds that you've spent your life building and then you are able to pass the wealth to your heirs. Therefore, in your golden years, you do not need protection in the form of life insurance. What you need when you retire is warm fluffy money; it's only cold hard cash when you don't have any.

To summarize, life insurance is needed as protection when you are young to provide for your family in case you prematurely pass on and everybody passes on prematurely. Retirement funds, not insurance, are needed for your retirement years but I don't like putting all my eggs in one basket.

If there is one thing you remember from this book, I hope it is this: The purpose of life insurance is NOT to build a savings account for your retirement or avoid income taxes. It can be used to safe guard you estate.

Unfortunately, many people buy these types of programs, such as universal life, hoping to combine an insurance policy with a retirement plan. These universal cash value life insurances are always terrible because you risk your retirement and income protection in one vehicle.

You should buy term insurance when you are young and later buy whole life and borrow out the cash value and invest it in real estate notes.

I say buy term before you have built up any real money in a retirement plan because you can buy twice as much term for half as much as cash value insurance. And invest in a retirement plan. If you die your family's needs are high because you have a mortgage, debt, kids' education and the spouse need money for retirement. When you're older you need whole life because your investments might not have grown the way you planned so if you die your spouse needs some of that warm fluffy money. You don't want to reach age 65 and have your retirement funds lose half their value and not have any insurance because your term policy's term was up.

Tom is a 37 year old male in Austin, TX who does not smoke and is in good health but he doesn't have much money. Tom has a whole life policy that he pays $120/month into. It gives him a life insurance policy for $100,000 and a cash value of $10,200 when he turns 65.

Do you see how combining insurance with retirement planning is a bad investment? Allow me to illustrate further why universal cash value life insurance is always a horrible investment. There is 1 major thing wrong with universal cash value insurance. The cost of insurance goes up every year inside the policy. If you have a universal life policy look at the guaranteed cost of insurance page and you will see that the cost of each $1,000 of insurance goes up every year. So if you were paying $5.00 per thousand when you were 45 at 65 you may be paying $20. The cost of insurance goes up every year but the payments you send in every month stays the same. The insurance company takes the extra amount out of your cash value and charges you interest.

If you had a $100,000 when you were 45 and paying $80 per month then $50 (100 X $5.00) went to pay for your insurance and *some* of the rest of the $30 went to your cash value account. At age 65 your insurance cost is now (100 X $20) $200. You are only paying $80 so the insurance company goes into your cash value and lends you your own money and charges you interest. Every month they are pulling out $120 and every year that number grows. Soon you have borrow out all of your cash value. You will get a notice that looks something like this. You no long have sufficient funds in your cash value account to keep this policy in force. To continue your coverage please pay your new premium of $750 per month.

You just spent most of your life and a lot of your money to end up with nothing.

In summery the universal life insurance companies keeps all the money for the first few years, you have to borrow the money from them and pay them interest, you either lose money are make very little and if you die they keep your money. Do you want to sign up for that?

Folks, these are insurance companies. This is why you don't invest your retirement account with them. They don't own skyscrapers in every major city because they give you the money.

There are ways to make whole life insurance advantages because whole life does not pay a return on your cash value, whole life can insure you in your later years which can be a great tax advantage and collateralize your money so that you can pick where to invest it. I'm happy to recommend insurance policies that are best for your circumstance. Just contact me at jw@JW Academy.com.

HOW MUCH INSURANCE DO YOU NEED?

Few agents know how to calculate how much insurance people need. The insurance industry uses something they call the DIME system; if you die your family needs enough to pay the **D**ebt, replace the **I**ncome, pay off the **M**ortgage and pay to **E**ducate the kids. Their formula a few years ago was to multiply your income times 8 so if you made $50,000 a year you needed $320,000 I mean $400,000 worth of insurance. After 3 or 4 years the industry number changed to 10 times your income. The change had nothing to do with how much insurance you needed. The insurance industry, after doing an exhaustive study, realized that insurance agents could not multiply by 8. Whether they multiplied by 8 or 10, it still didn't have anything to do with how much you owed, how much your mortgage payment was or how many kids you were sending to college. You are paying all of these things with your current income so common sense tells you that you only need to replace your income.

Use your common sense and decide which method makes more sense. Joe and Mary want to pay their mortgage, pay their debt, save for their kids' education and for their own retirement. They are using their current incomes to do all of these things. Joe makes $3,000 per month and Mary makes $1,750 per month. If Joe were to die how much of his income will Mary need, to pay the mortgage, pay their debt, fund the kid's education and save for her retirement? The answer is all of it. Mary would need some way to replace $3,000 per month. If she can't do that, she will pay the mortgage, she will pay the debt and she will send the kids to collage but she will have to work until she drops dead because she won't have enough money to save for her retirement.

Life insurance is to replace income so she needs enough insurance to replace $3,000. I believe that a 7% return is obtainable(real estate notes) so Joe needs to have enough insurance so that if he dies Mary can invest the proceeds at 7% and withdraw $3,000 per month without decreasing the principal. Here is a simple formula to calculate the needed amount. Multiply Joe's income of $3,000 per month by 172. Example $3,000 X 172 = $516,000. Joe needs $516,000 worth of insurance because if Mary invested $516,000 in something that made 7% she could take out $2,992 per month and never reduce the principal I've known Joe a long time and can assure you he drinks at least $8 worth of beer a month so $2,992 will be enough cause when Joe dies he will finally quit drinking. So you can multiply your monthly income by 172 and you will know how much insurance to buy. Since I have never meet an insurance agent that knew how to calculate how much insurance you need, don't trust their system. My system makes sense doesn't it? Common Sense.

PAYING OFF DEBT

Since the name of this book is "***How to Save Money Even If You're Broke!"*** We need to look at the number one thing that makes us broke—**debt**.

It confused me why debt seems to be so much worse now than it has been, even in the very resent past. Until the 1920s there were very few mortgages and they were mostly 10 year. There was no such thing as a true credit card until about 1979. Credit and debt are an overarching theme of American life. Today, an American family carries an average of eight different credit cards, and debt levels that are climbing. Americans embrace the idea of "buy now, pay later," but how did this virus of payment by credit begin? Merchants loved accepting cards because customers tended to spend more today when using credit cards.

On average, customers spend approximately 112% more when using credit cards than they do when using cash. Common sense tells us that if we spend 112% more of our money and don't make 112% more money, someday there will be TROUBLE. For banks, credit cards were a source of constant revenue via interest charges to customers and fees paid by merchants. It's easy to see why banks advertised for people to use credit cards; no matter what you buy with your credit card and no matter where you buy it, the bank gets to participate in the profit.

How did we the people get hooked on credit cards? The answer is **gradually**. It has been argued that Rasputin helped to discredit the tsarist government, leading to the fall of the Czar, in 1917 Russia. Rasputin knew he had many enemies who wanted him dead, so every day he would take a very small drop of cyanide. After a few years he gradually built up immunity to cyanide. Sure enough his enemies tried to poison him but it had no effect so they shot him 4 times and then drowned him. I believe the banks hooked us on those cyanide credit cards. Gradually we just accepted them as a way of life. Now they are trying to drown us.

Debt's a Bitch

Secrets are hard to keep. How have the rich been so good at it? Why do the poor generally stay poor? The philosopher Jim Rohn said the secret to being wealthy is to watch what the poor people do and don't do that. Can it be that simple? I think so. The following is what I have seen poor people do and have done myself. Using some things I have observed, I will share some simple ways to do what rich people do.

In the book, The Secret, we are told to just visualize whatever you want and it will **manifest** itself. Well Bull! If that were true I could think myself a full head of hair. Visualizing and manifesting might work with rich people because they have the money to buy whatever they want. In my case, a hair transplant. But us average Americans can stand in our garden and say, "There are no weeds, there are no weeds, there are no weeds" and the weeds will take over our garden. You must take action to remove the weeds. Most of us don't take action. We accept the most commonly accepted financial advice that's out there. We all probably just missed a few words in The Secret. We thought that it said "borrow the money for whatever you want and it will manifest itself," not visualize.

Debt's a Bitch

To hell with political correctness, from now on I'll just call it like I see it and I have confidence you can sort it out. Debt controls our lives. Those four words need to be bigger. **DEBT CONTROLS OUR LIVES**. They need to be as big as the Hollywood sign on the hill overlooking Hollywood, California. Our debt controls when we go to work, where we work, who we work for, how much we work, whether we enjoy our work, when we can quit working and the quality of life when we retire from work. It controls where our kids go to school, the type of school they go to and the amount of money they owe when they graduate. Since debt controls how much we work, it also controls how much time we can spend with our families and the quality of our lives.

There are direct links between debt and our health, both physical and mental. I believe debt causes us to make bad decisions based on the fact that we have to make a payment on our mortgage or a credit card. Debt can shake your faith, end your marriage and hold your sleep hostage. Debt's a BITCH!

Forty years ago the way to figure what something cost you was simple. The cost of something was whatever you walked into a store and paid. Today all that has changed; the cost of something is whatever it cost you. I know, that's confusing but since most of us pay for things with credit cards we pay much more for everything we buy. Would you buy a TV for $1,500? You probably would but would you pay $2,300 for the same TV at another store? Well, if you charged that TV, it'll cost you $2,300. My definition of a fool is someone who lies to themselves and believes it. I could break down the math and show you the formulas but you already know the way things work. What you don't know is a way to get out of debt because if you knew a way to get out of debt you would not be in debt.

▪ Debt

I'm sure you've heard that old saying "If life gives you a lemon; make lemonade." I'm also sure what I am about to say is counter intuitive. The more debt you are now paying on, the more money you will have when you retire. That is if you get a Financial Blueprint and follow it. The reason for this anomaly is simple (I know I use that word a lot but I'm a simple guy); all the money you are using to pay all that debt with is money you are not using to live on. You live on what is left over after you pay your debt. Do you know what you pay with to work where you work; your life.

Once we do a Financial Blueprint for you we will find you some money to get that debt paid off. So the more you are paying now, the sooner you will be able to pay your debt off. The sooner you pay it off the sooner you can start redirecting that large amount of money you were spending on debt and now you can use it to invest.

If the example Financial Blueprint I showed you earlier had $20,000 more debt and he paid $800 a month instead of $489, he would retire with $988,884 instead of $890,976. That's almost $100,000 more because he had $20,000 more in debt.

Don't forget that when you do a Financial Blueprint it doesn't change your cash flow. You are being much more efficient with your money. Doesn't that make more sense than cutting back on the joys of life and depriving your family and yourself of things that you all enjoy? There it is again common sense.

▪ That "Out of Debt Feeling"

One of the best warm fuzzy feelings you will ever have is when you take the first step toward getting out of debt. The pride you will feel at finally moving toward something that you now know is easily obtainable will not only push you to keep going, but will pull you with a force even bad habits can't stop. With each small step you will make a quantum leap toward financial freedom. You have the right to feel pride when you understand the power that you've gained to take control of your family's future.

That first increase in your pay check you get because you started a part-time business and lower your income tax will work miracles for your self-esteem. Once that additional money pays off the first credit card, you will never want to go deeper in debt. The first one is always the hardest but with our help, the time will be short. The second, third, fourth and so on will fly by until the day you can say the words that few before you have ever said, "I've paid off all my credit cards." Using your new found discipline and freed up cash you will be confident that you now have the ability to pay your house off in only a few more years.

To still be young and have a paid for a house is very rare. Now you have enough money and time to build up a huge retirement fund. To be able to retire when you wish and do whatever you want <u>for the rest of your life</u> without any money worries is the greatest gift you can give your family, your health and yourself.

▪ It's Not Your Fault

I said it before and I will say it again **it's not your fault.**

I heard a story about two African tribes were about to fight a battle. They lined up across from each other and the strongest warrior from one tribe went out in front of his army and taunted the other tribe. The other tribe did not have a mighty warrior to send out, but they did have a renowned witch doctor to send out. All the tribes believe that this witch doctor was very powerful. He moved in close to the powerful warrior and pointed a stick at him. The witch doctor sited a curse of death and pointed the stick at the warrior who dropped dead on the spot. You and I both know that the stick had no power other than the power that the warrior himself gave it. His very beliefs killed him.

The credit bureaus are very similar to the Voodoo stick in that the power they have is mostly in your head.

▪ The FICO God

I named this "The FICO God" after the name of the company that determines if we get credit and what we are charged. I saw someone pray to FICO, the God of credit, in Wal-Mart the other day. A woman in front of me at the checkout counter slide her credit card, closed her eyes, bowed her head and prayed, "Please, Please, PLEASE!" When she opened her eyes, first one then the other the FICO God answered her prayer, "APPROVED." She then looked up and mouthed the words "thank you."

A long, long, long time ago (actually it was in the 70's) when a man's word was his bond, there were no credit bureaus. The only way a lender had to check how you paid your debt was to call someplace that you had charged something and ask the merchant how you paid. As more and more people started buying on time the merchant had to start answering more and more calls; soon it became a large expense to hire someone to answer all the inquiries. We are a very litigious society and many of the merchant were getting sued for reporting that the customer didn't pay very well. Some diabolical genius came up with a cunning plan. He started the first credit bureau. The purpose of a credit bureau was to act as a buffer between the merchants and the customers. The merchants could fire the person that they hired to answer all those credit inquiries and only pay the credit bureau a small fee each month. The credit bureau would also act as a buffer between the customers and the merchants. This is the way it began and it grew into the monster it is today.

The banks and other lending institutions then saw a way to use the credit bureaus to increase their profits. Lenders never wanted to refuse anybody credit, they simply wanted to be able to charge the people a lot more interest. Two men named Fair and Isaac came up with a scoring system they named after themselves the Fair Isaac Corporation or as you know it FICO. I promise you, there is nothing fair about the Fair Isaac Corp.

The banks, lenders and insurance companies use the low FICO score to get people to accept paying a higher interest or a higher premium than people with higher scores paid. If the people with the lower FICO scores complained, they were told, "There is nothing we can do about your rate because you're FICO score dictates what you pay." How conveeenient. It's like saying that the cost you must pay is not our fault the FICO God has chosen your fate and rate.

They have taken away your name and given you a number. Merle Haggard has a song called 'Branded Man' which describes it perfectly. "I've paid the debt I owe them, but they're not satisfied now I'm a branded man out in the cold." They've taken away my name and given me a number. These credit bureaus have branded us with a number that means more than our name. This brand now controls almost everything we do and everything our children will do. It drives us to drugs, alcohol, lying, stealing, divorce, humiliation, depression and desperation. It is eroding our capitalist system and is stealing our liberty.

Do you know why the credit bureaus reports bankruptcies for 10 years and bad credit for 7? They do it because they want to. There is no law that requires them to track these things for any time, just a law that lets them. The average prison term for manslaughter is 15 months; you'll get 7 years for one bill 30 days past due.

In America, you are innocent until proven guilty. All the things on your credit are accusations - for them to remain they must be proven and that's a hard thing to do. The only way the credit bureau can keep bad things on your report is to make it almost impossible to contact them directly. Every time you do what they tell you to do they change the procedure; you waste a lot of time and energy and finally give up. THAT'S THE SIMPLE PLAN!

The credit bureaus are literally depriving you of your Constitutional Right to life, liberty and the pursuit of happiness.

They do not get their power from laws but act like Gods. They make the laws up themselves and keep them secret from the public. If you ask for verification on an item in your bureau, they simply send you a form letter that they have verified the item and it will remain. You can't find or afford a lawyer who will take these FICO Gods on. The only way to stop them is to let your Congressmen know that this is important to you and you want something done. There should be a law that makes it illegal for bad credit to stay on your record for more than 2 years and a 30 days late for no longer than 6 months. When a late payment is made up, it should be removed. When you paid the debt you owe them, they should be satisfied but the FICO God is vengeful. Nobody knows how credit scores are calculated and the credit bureaus keep their formulas secret. Your credit score is your property and they should not be able to take your property without due process.

We also have a "Simple Plan" at financial Blueprinting; we show you how to get completely out of debt without effecting your cash flow in a very few years. Once we get you out of debt, and that includes your home, you don't need a FICO score. You will have something much more powerful than the FICO God, you will have CASH!

There is a law of Diminishing Intent so when you finish this you need to do something; either delete it or contact me JW at jw@JWAcademy.com .

▪ MORTGAGE CANCER

With all the turmoil in the mortgage business lately the conventional wisdom is to buy a 15 year or 30 year fixed rate mortgage. Suddenly the mortgage industry is going to look after you.

The word mortgage is derived from the Latin word 'mort,' which means death and from the German word 'gage' which means pledge. Cancer is something evil or malignant that spreads destructively. There is no other way to describe how a fixed rate, 30 year mortgage works other than a pledge to die by an evil or malignant cancer that spreads destructively.

Would you buy a house with a 116% interest rate for $150,000 with a monthly payment of $899.33 for 30 years that will cost you a total of $323,748? The problem is that most people have said yes to that last question. What you have just read is not a car loan, payday loan, or a loan from a loan shark; it's an actual 30 year, 6% fixed rate mortgage. A mortgage of $150,000.00 at 6% for 30 years with a monthly payment of $899 will cost you $323,640. You'll pay $150,000 principal and $173,640 interest.

The only thing fixed about a fixed rate mortgage is the payment. I know you signed a contract to pay 6%, but that's not exactly what you paid. If you would like a very simple formula to calculate what your real interest was or is at any time in your mortgage, just divide the principal into the interest. For example $173,640(Interest) divided by $150,000 (Principal). That mean for every $1 you spent on principal you spent $1.16 on interest. To put it simply your interest rate is 116% not 6%. Would you have bought the house if you had known the interest rate was 116%? Most people will unwittingly go out and do this over and over and over and over again with 30 year fixed rate loans. <u>*Times Change, A Nickel is Just Not Worth a Dime Anymore*</u>

How to Calculate Mortgage Interest

I can work a financial calculator as good as the best and I was trying to figure out how mortgage companies calculated amortization interest. No matter how hard I tried or who I asked, I could not understand how they calculated the interest until one day at Taco

Cabana. I was at Taco Cabana to meet a friend of mine for lunch. He was late so I was just sitting there thinking (obsessing) about interest rates. I didn't bring my calculator with me so I was just thinking when it hit me. What I really wanted to know was for every dollar of principal spent in a loan, how many dollars of interest was paid? If I borrow $100 and paid back $110 I would divide the principal into the interest and that would tell me the REAL interest rate. $10 divided by $100 = .10 or 10%.

I had been working on this problem trying to use a financial calculator and conventional wisdom for a month. When I applied a little common sense, it didn't take long to figure out. A $150,000 mortgage for 30 years with a 6% interest and a payment of $899.33 the first payment $149.33 is applied to principal reduction and $750 is applied to interest. I divided $750 by $149.33 and realized that for every dollar spent on principal $5.02 was spent on interest. That's 502% interest.

It is very easy for lenders to sell fixed rate mortgages if they don't have to disclose the actual rate. Truth in Lending is an oxymoron. Conventional wisdom tells people that these are good mortgages. The lenders put the highest interest up front; this is called front-end loaded. A 6% 30 year mortgage starts at 502% and after 30 years it dropped to 116%. The reason is simple, most people move every 5 years. When you sell your home, you still owe the remaining principal. After half the loan you have only paid 25% of the principle. This is called the rule of 50/25 when you have paid half of the payments you have only reduced your principal by a quarter

Here is an amortization table on a 30 year fixed rate loan calculated with common sense. . There is only simple interest and simple principal reduction. You have never heard of anyone charging complicated interest have you? When you combine simple interest with simple principal reduction you get something that is not simple it's called amortization.

EXAMPLE:

Mortgage	**$ 150,000**
Interest Rate	**6.00%**
Payment Principal & Interest	**$ 899.33**

Regular Mortgage

first	Interest	Principal	Balance	Cost I-P
month	750.00	149.33	149,850.67	***$5.02***

Yr. #	Cumulative Interest	Cumulative Principal	Ending Balance	Cost Int. to Prin.
1	8,949.89	1,842.02	148,157.98	$4.86
2	17,786.17	3,797.65	146,202.35	$4.68
3	26,501.83	5,873.89	144,126.11	$4.51
4	35,089.44	8,078.20	141,921.80	$4.34
5	43,541.08	10,418.46	139,581.54	***$4.18***
6	51,848.39	12,903.07	137,096.93	$4.02
7	60,002.45	15,540.92	134,459.08	$3.86
8	67,993.81	18,341.47	131,658.53	$3.71
9	75,812.44	21,314.75	128,685.25	$3.56
10	83,447.68	24,471.41	125,528.59	$3.41
11	90,888.23	27,822.77	122,177.23	$3.27
12	98,122.07	31,380.84	118,619.16	$3.13
13	105,136.47	35,158.36	114,841.64	$2.99
14	111,917.87	39,168.87	110,831.13	$2.86
15	118,451.91	43,426.73	106,573.27	$2.73
16	124,723.33	47,947.22	102,052.78	$2.60
17	130,715.95	52,746.51	97,253.49	$2.48
18	136,412.55	57,841.82	92,158.18	$2.36
19	141,794.88	63,251.40	86,748.60	$2.24
20	146,843.57	68,994.62	81,005.38	$2.13
21	151,538.02	75,092.08	74,907.92	$2.02
22	155,856.40	81,565.61	68,434.39	$1.91
23	159,775.50	88,438.41	61,561.59	$1.81
24	163,270.71	95,735.12	54,264.88	$1.71
25	166,315.87	103,481.87	46,518.13	$1.61
26	168,883.22	111,706.42	38,293.58	$1.51
27	170,943.31	120,438.25	29,561.75	$1.42
28	172,464.83	129,708.63	20,291.37	$1.33
29	173,414.58	139,550.79	10,449.21	$1.24
30	173,757.28	150,000.00	0.00	$1.16
	173,757.28	**150,000**	**TOTALS**	***116%***

ESSENTIALS

We do everything we do for reasons. Since everything we do is for a reason then reasons are indeed essentials. I know that when I was in high school I didn't want a job; I wanted money so I could do things on the weekends. Because it was one of my highest priorities, it was essential to me. As I grew older my reasons changed and so other things became essential.

If you want to make a change in your personal finances, then make only slight changes in your financial habits. I'm not suggesting, like other financial gurus do, that you go on a 'beans and rice' financial diet, because these types of diets don't work. It's too hard to keep up long term, and you just fall back into the same trap you were trying to leave in the beginning. Financial diets don't work any better than food diets. I've seen those "before and after" diet ads and even tried a few myself—but I could use the same picture for before and after.

You've been spending most of your money on Taxes, Insurance and Debt which left very little for the Essentials like gas, food, kids' education and saving for retirement, you know the essentials. What I have done so far is show you a way to reduce the cost of your Taxes, Insurance and Debt and use the money for Essentials and Savings.

▪ SAVINGS

Smile, saving money is much easier than you think. You don't need much money; a simple change can start growing your savings accounts, even if you're broke. Without affecting your life style, suddenly you will be telling your friend a whole new story. Can you imagine what that will feel like?

All of the things you are about to read are simply my common sense conclusions to all the conventional wisdom we have been fed for most of our lives. I spent 20 years as a different type of financial advisor; most advisors advise people where to put their money. I showed people where to find the money. Most experts use "Conventional Wisdom" as the guide to where to invest; I use "Common Sense" to make that decision. When I first wrote the rough draft of this book I described in detail where not to put your money, then I revealed where I thought was the best place to put your money. After I thought about that for a while I came to this conclusion "this is a book about finance; there is no hero, beautiful girls or a cute little alien named Paul." I suspected very few people will read the whole thing so I need to put in what I think is the best place to invest your money here." Once you have made the rather simple decision of where to put your money then I will show you a very simple and easy to understand system for finding the money to invest. Last, but not least, I will describe why the "Conventional Wisdom'" investments stink.

▪ High Interest Savings

In the movie The Jerk when Bernadette Peters and Steve Martin had gone broke, she said, and I quote, "It's not the money I'll miss; it's the STUFF." If you use our Financial Blueprint you don't have to give up the STUFF; we show you how to find the money in places that you have been forced to spend it like taxes, insurance and debt. That makes us different from any financial advisor you have ever talked to.

Once you have found the money to invest by reducing your taxes, making insurance tax deductible and then use the freed up money to quickly pay off your debt. Now you need to invest your freed up cash in something that has two major components. One: it must pay a guaranteed interest. Two: it must be backed by collateral. Saving money is great, but you have to make it not just work for you but it must work hard for you. If you put $50,000 in a CD for 10 years at 2% you will only have made $1,060, that's just $8.83 a month. The Mommas and the Pappas had a song that said, "Nobody's getting fat except Momma Cass;" well, nobody's getting fat with CDs except the banks. The banks borrow your money and pay you peanuts, then they lend it back out and charge an arm and a leg. As my Dad used to say, "That dog don't hunt." You can do better and you know it! Never think savings is like the "Dancing Bear" at the circus; it's not that the bear dances well, it's just that it dances. Just saving money isn't the big thing; making a high return on your money is the big thing.

You want to earn money on your savings? The Richest Man in Babylon describes the key to wealth as treating your money like workers; put them to work, and put their children (interest) to work, and their children's children and etc.... In other words, make your money earn money in the form of guaranteed interest, and make that interest earn additional interest.

Compound interest is the secret to wealth creation! The difference between simple interest and compound interest can be explained like this: simple interest is simply interest rate multiplied times principal (example; 10% simple interest on $10,000 is $1,000 no matter how long) while compound interest adds the interest to the principal each month. Adding the interest to the principal each month gives you more principal in which to earn interest, which leads to more savings! (Example: 10% compounded interest for 10 years on $10,000 = $27,070.)

Given this type of strategy, finding a higher interest program is paramount. Common sense tells you just about all you need to know about which interest is best for you, high and collateralized.

▪ Real Estate Notes the Best Place to Invest

I believe that real estate notes are the best place to save for your retirement. They pay a high fixed interest rate, there is good collateral, you can diversify and compound your investment, you don't pay property taxes, you don't pay maintenance, you don't pay property insurance and you get paid every month. That is why all the big banks like them so much.

You know what I'm talking about if you have ever bought a house; within a few months you get a notice that your mortgage has been sold. Your contract remains the same except you now send your payments to a new address. What you were seeing was a bank bought your mortgage from the original lender at a discount. Because the buying bank paid less than the amount of the note they will in reality receives a higher interest rate than the original note was contracted for. The new bank now gets paid with a high fixed interest rate, with great collateral and very, very low expenses. Remember they are the lender so they don't pay for maintenance, property taxes or insurance. When you buy an owner financed mortgage you have as collateral a first lien. The original lender has already qualified the owner and trusted them enough to lend the money. The original lender was lending their own personal money so they made sure that the loan to value was good. When you buy the mortgage, someone else has already done the work. Don't you wish you could buy into something like that? You can.

▪ Real Estate Conventional Wisdom

Conventional Wisdom tells you that real estate is a safe place to put your money. But mark this down—how you invest in real estate is more important than where you invest. There are literally thousands of mentors and educational groups who will teach you how to buy real estate, how to flip it, how to finance it and how to fix it up to market it. It seems to me that if there is so much money in doing all these things and there is only a limited supply of suitable properties the people who know how to do it would pay to keep you from finding out their secrets. So logically they can make more money teaching you than they can by doing it themselves; it's only common sense. You are most likely not interested in starting all over in a new profession (real estate investor) and simply want to get a good return on your money. Owner financed mortgages are just that—they are a high return. Remember you are not buying real estate, you are buying a mortgage.

▪ Owner Financed Mortgages

The new paradigm is the purchase of real estate notes. Owner financed mortgages are becoming the best option to save for retirement because they offer a fixed interest rate on your money and you can buy them for as little as $7,000. An owner financed mortgage is simply created by someone who wants to sell their house, but can't find anyone who can qualify or they would like a steady income from the property. The owner might run an ad in the newspaper that states, "House for sale $100,000 owner will finance with $10,000 down @ 11%." The buyer does not have to have a highest credit score or any of the other hoops that today's lenders make people jump through. The payments will be $857.09 for 30 years. After 5 years the original owner may want to simply get his money now and is willing to sell the note for less than the $87,448 that is still owed on the note. You've probably heard the ad on TV "It's my money and I want it now." The purchaser of the mortgage will pay $84,448 for an $87,448 mortgage. The collateral is a $100,000 house.

Today there are 10,000 baby boomers retiring every day. There are also about that many of the baby boomers' parents that are dying and leaving the boomers houses that they don't want to live in. It's not easy to find a bank that will lend money on these under $100,000 houses or for that matter any house. It costs a bank just as much to do a $100,000 loan as a $350,000 and they make a lot more money on the $350,000 house, plus people who buy $100,000 houses generally don't have as good of credit as the upper end buyers. Owner financed mortgages are the solution to these boomers. It's very easy to sell an owner financed house. I was talking to a man in south Texas, Joe Flores, who told me that he had been trying to sell a house with no luck until one day he put a sign in the front yard "For Sale, Owner Financing." Before he could get 10 miles from the house he got his first of many calls. He turned around and met the buyers back at the house and sold it.

▪ What's Changed in Owner Financed Mortgages?

The first things you need to know about the Conventional Wisdom on note buying are the huge drawbacks the old way of buying notes has.

1. You have to have a large amount of money to buy a note
2. You have to locate someone willing to sell you their note
3. You have to collect the payments and late fees
4. You have all your eggs in one basket
5. You can't compound your interest

The good Common Sense things are:

1. You are not the landlord so you don't have to fix things
2. You are the lien holder so you don't pay property tax

3. You don't pay for the insurance
4. You don't pay maintenance
5. You don't deal with a lot of people moving in and out
6. You get paid a fixed interest rate
7. Your taxes are lower because some of the payment is return of principal
8. You can make this your self-directed IRA
9. You can make this a savings type account
10. You can use the payments for cash flow or you can reinvest and compound your interest

I think that if you are going to invest in property, you will need to change the way you look at houses; you are not buying a mortgage on a house that you are going to live in. You are buying a mortgage on a house that will give you the most safety and the highest return on your investment dollar.

▪ Lesson From Pop

As I look back to the summers I spent with my grandfather in Longview Texas, I realize that almost everything he did was to teach me something that would serve me later in life. I called my grandfather Pop. Pop had an old green Studebaker pickup and a new long white Cadillac. He also owned a bunch of small rent houses. He would take me with him in that old, no air Studebaker truck to pick up the all the rent payments. He told me that he would rather have 10 low rent houses than one high rent house. He said, "JW, if the economy gets bad there will be a big demand for low rent houses and if the economy gets good there is still a big demand for low rent houses." These houses were scattered all over Gregg County Texas. My father was a car salesman and Pop told me that when you buy a car it cost you money and it becomes less valuable, but when you buy a house and rent it out it makes you money and it becomes more valuable. I'd say Pop knew what he was talking about.

There are a lot of people these days that know what Pop taught me is true, but they live paycheck to paycheck and never have enough money to buy income property. Many spend thousands going to Rich Dad Poor Dad programs to learn how to buy income property but few ever get it done; the property is hard to find, expensive to finance and can be very risky. There are just too many headaches associated with being a landlord, but Pop still had a good idea. The idea was to put your money in something that paid a fixed amount and was backed by collateral.

If you have tried all of the "No Money Down Plans" and recognized that if you could just get started, passive income from real estate is much better than risking you hard-earned money in the unstable stock market, well finally there is a common sense answer—purchase owner financed mortgages.

I'm sure if Pop would have known about Owner Financed Mortgages he would have liked them more than rental income property. The advantages are clear no, maintenance, no taxes and no insurance expense.

I think you now know what real estate notes are, now I will show you the risks involved, the growth potential and the mechanics of how to purchase notes. You will see why banks love to buy mortgages.

Real Estate Notes (Owner Financed Mortgages) the New Paradigm

A real estate note is just another name for a mortgage, so you should just think of them as mortgages from now. You have heard of buying mortgages, even if it didn't register with you at the time. As I said before, if you have ever bought a house, the odds are within a few months you got a notice that someone had bought your mortgage, all the terms remain the same except you will now mail your check to a different address.

The definition of the word paradigm is "one that serves as a pattern or model." As I sat here thinking of the best way to describe something I would call a new way of thinking about retirement planning, I looked at my wrist watch and noticed that it was made in Switzerland. Up until about 1970 the Swiss controlled 90% of the watch industry. Everybody knew that if the watch had a Swiss movement it was a quality product. The Swiss had a paradigm or belief of what a watch was; it was a high quality, precision, elegant, jeweled, statement of who the wearer was. James Bond wore a Rolex.

The Swiss watch makers were always trying to improve on their product and one day saw the digital clock invented by a NASA engineer named Peter Dimitroff, who came up with the idea of a digital quartz wrist watch. This was a very accurate time piece, but it certainly wasn't high quality, precision, elegant, jeweled, statement of who the wearer was. It did not fit the Swiss paradigm of a wrist watch.

The Swiss thought it was cute, but they saw no great demand for it because it did not fit their paradigm. The technology was shown at a World's Fair where three other companies were. Seiko, Bulova and Texas Instruments saw the digital watch and got excited. They got excited because they knew what the Swiss thought a watch was, but they also knew what the rest of the world thought the purpose of a watch was. They knew that the rest of the world really saw a wrist watch as "something on your wrist that told you what time it was." Today the Swiss only have about 10% of the market. They refused to change their paradigm until it was too late.

I know you are wondering why I told you that story. I did it so you would open your mind to a new idea, a new paradigm of how a retirement plan should work. Most people want to retire and keep living as well as they have been. They want to go where they want to go and do what they want to do. Most like to invest where everybody they know invests; mutual funds in their 401k. They want to make sure that when they retire they still have enough warm fluffy cash flow to enjoy their retirement. Nobody wants to work hard all their life and retire broke. Most people are not interested in becoming financial experts or day traders, they simply want to have enough money to stop working and start enjoying their life at some time.

I remember back in 1960 my dad got one of the first cars with a cruise control. He told me that on a long trip he would set the cruise control at 70 mph and just put his feet up on the dash. Most people put a few bucks in a 401k and spend the rest of their working life with their feet up on the dash. Both of these examples sound a little dangerous to me.

I will go into how the old retirement plan paradigms like investing your money in mutual funds, gold, insurance policies or CDs later. You probably already understand how unstable or unprofitable they can be. You have put your money where the so-called retirement experts have told you to and then you put your feet up on the dash. How's that working? You need a new paradigm.

▪ Risk

So we should look at the risks that come with buying an Owner Financed Mortgage and the ways to reduce that risk. There is a risk that people won't make their payments. If you can't work something out with them you can take the property. Since the original note was below the assessed value of the property and you bought that note at a discount you are in a much better financial position than if you had stock in GM. So the risk of loss is minimized. If you have to resell the house, you can sell it much easier than other homes in the area because you can offer owner financing and you get a down payment. Don't forget Joe the gentleman from south Texas.

▪ Growth Potential

If you will buy a lot of little notes you have diversified, which also lowers the risk of loss.

Einstein said the most powerful force in the universe was compound interest. He didn't say interest was the most powerful force in the universe, he said compound interest was the most powerful force in the universe. People have been buying owner financed mortgages for years, but until now they didn't know how to compound their interest. Using the example below if you bought the Kyle mortgage for $19,669 you would receive $247.02 per month. If you put that $247.02 in a money market account in less than 3 years you will have enough to buy the property in Dallas for $8,900 that would pay you another $129.53 per month. You would still be getting the $247.02 from Kyle so that's $376.55 per month. In 23.7 months you could buy another house like Kyle's and each month you would collect $506.08

per month which gives you enough in 17.6 months to get another. That's the power of compounding.

Let me give you some examples of some notes and the money that can be made.

If you had $50,000 in your 401k or IRA and used the money to purchase owner financed mortgages as shown above you would be collecting $715.68 per month. In about 12 months, you could buy an $8,900 note like the one in Dallas. You would then receive $845.21 per month and in 10.5 months you could buy another. Isn't common sense profitable?

▪ How to Purchase Owner Financed Mortgages

I know of no other company that works this way other than Realbridge Solutions. Contact Mandy Hanks at 866-612-1604, or go to www.RealbridgeSolutions.com, or you can sent them an email at info@RealbridgeSolution.com. If you send Realbridge Solutions a request, they will send you a list of current mortgages you can buy and a free calculator to see which ones fit you best. You pay no fees; Realbridge is paid by the seller.

The Banks Don't Pay You to Save With Them, They Charge You.

The guaranteed interest rate is not free. Historically banks have always made most of their money by borrowing money from depositors and paying them a very low rate and then lending the same money back out and charging a much higher rate. There is nothing wrong with this system because it was very easy to compare one bank to another by simple comparing interest rates. But banks learned that they could make a lot more people deposit money with them by paying a higher rate and making up the difference by putting fees in on everything. They then could pay a higher interest rate and more than make up the difference with fees. They would only advertise their high rates.

Lately I have been watching a TV series call pawn stores, which shows people bringing in things they want to pawn. When the owners don't know what something is worth they bring in an expert to put a value on it. The expert not only tells the pawn shop owner the value of the product, but he also tells the customer. If the item is worth $3,000, the pawn shop owner will offer about $1,500. The customer understands that the pawn shop has to make money on the sale. Everybody knows the way an honest business works. A pawn shop is up front with what they are doing, a bank however hides what is actually going on. Banks make you think you are getting one thing but you are getting something else. I think I can explain how banks charge you for the guaranteed interest they supposedly pay you.

Einstein's Rule of 72 tells you how long it takes for your money to double at any interest rate. You simply divide the interest rate into 72. Examples: 10% ÷ 72 = 7.2 years, 1.5% ÷ 72= 48 years,. How many 48 year stretches do you have left in your life?

If you put $2,000 in a bank that pays you 1.5% at age 19 by age 67 (48 years) you will have $4,000. You made $2,000 in 48 years.

If you put $2,000 into notes that averaged 10% you would have $238,000. You made $236,000.

Since banks lend money, issue credit cards and buy notes, they take your $2,000 and make at least 10%, in 48 years they have $238,000, they pay you your $4,000 and keep the rest. They charged you $234,000 for a 1.5% guarantee. That works out to $406 per month that they charged you to guarantee you 1.5% interest. They charge you $406 per month on a $2,000 deposit. Sometimes common sense is painful knowledge.

COMMON SENSE SAVINGS FOR RETIREMENT

I feel that letting a financial planner control your retirement funds by blindly investing in the stock market, annuities, gold, CDs or cash value insurance is a strategy that not only died many years ago but was tortured to death and has begun to stink. It's time for you to take control.

So where should you invest for your future? Conventional wisdom says to invest it and leave it alone.

I understand how annuities, life insurance, mutual funds, commodities, stocks, money markets and CDs work and would never put my money in them. Only put your money in things **you understand** after you've done some research yourself. Your common sense will keep you out of trouble. "Never trust someone you shouldn't trust; you know who they are."

I had a friend who was a car salesman tell me that he was very excited about the new pay plan that the owner had worked on for weeks. He said that it would be a great raise. I informed him that if the owner wanted to give his sales force a raise he wouldn't have to work on it for weeks; he could just give them a raise. Sure enough even after selling more cars the next month he made less money.

If you have ever bought an annuity, a cash value life insurance policy or a mutual fund I would bet a $100 to $1 you not only didn't read the contract or understand the rules. Seriously, if the annuity company was going to pay you 4% on your money they could say that in one sentence, why would the need 25 pages?

I was going to rent an office once and they faxed me over a 45 page lease. I didn't even read it because I knew that they were screwing me on at least 44 pages. These experts don't get to you because of the things you know; they get to you because of the things you **think you know**. The bold print gives and the fine print takes it away.

Remember that if your advisor is rich, he probably got that way selling people like you annuities, cash value insurance and mutual fund not investing in them.

▪ Savings for Retirement

The Grasshopper and the Ant

I was blessed this past Christmas to be able to have 3 generations of my family with me in my home. As any proud Grandparent can tell you, one of the most cherished moments of life is being able to sit in your favorite rocking chair by the fire, read bedtime stories to your grandchildren, and be able to pass along a lifetime of wisdom and lessons to their young, inquisitive minds. History has proved that if you want to teach a child or anyone something of great value, it is best taught in a story.

I was reading an Aesop's Fable to my grandsons the other night and was amazed how the lessons we learn as a child still apply today. But somehow, from the time we were 3 years old until the time we are senior citizens, we seem to forget some of these simple lessons. Here is a summary of the fable I read my grandchild called the Ant and the Grasshopper:

In a field one summer's day a Grasshopper was hopping about, chirping and singing to its heart's content. An Ant passed by, bearing along with great toil an ear of corn he was taking to the nest.

"Why not come and chat with me," said the Grasshopper, "instead of toiling and moiling in that way?"

"I am helping to lay up food for the winter," said the Ant, "and recommend you to do the same." "Why bother about winter?" said the Grasshopper; we have got plenty of food at present." But the Ant went on its way and continued its toil. When the winter came the Grasshopper had no food and found itself dying of hunger, while everyday it saw the ants distributing corn and grain from the stores they had collected in the summer. Then the Grasshopper knew it is best to prepare for the days of necessity. There is no greater pain than the pain of regret.

For most people, the days of necessity are during their retirement. But, unfortunately, like the grasshopper, most people fail to prepare in advance for this time. Prince did a song where he says, "I've seen the future and it's rough." But with more people living longer, expenses getting higher, debt eating up the only money that could be used for savings and fewer safe ways to save for retirement, procrastination can cripple you when winter comes. You do not want to be up a polluted tributary without means of propulsion (up Sh – t Creek without a paddle).

What causes procrastination? Generally, fear of the unknown. If you don't know how to grow your money, then you are less likely to try to save for retirement.

As I was reading to my grandsons, I began to think about what my grandparents and parents had taught me about money and the lessons that I had learned.

My first lesson about money started when I was about 5 years old. Pop, my grandfather had peanut vending machines and each Saturday, we would go around town to each of these machines putting in peanuts and taking out pennies. We would then go to the local bank and deposit the money, because Pop told me it was safe and that the bank would pay me guaranteed interest. "Guaranteed interest," my Grandfather would say, "was the most reliable way to grow money because you could actually plan to the penny what your money would be worth in the future." Pop had lived through the Great Depression and wasn't interested in 'gambling' with money, like many other had done through the stock market.

That money Pop and I collected every weekend from the peanut machines ended up paying for my college education years later.

As I grew older, saving money became more of a challenge. Like my Grandfather and many of you, I liked the idea of guaranteed interest, but my problem with banks was that the number in front of the percent sign was too small, so I began looking for other opportunities to make my money work for me.

I am a slow learner but very prideful; I don't admit mistakes easily. One day my dad was shoeing our horse. He was heating the shoes up red hot and bending them with a hammer to fit. When he had it right he just tossed them on the ground to cool. I saw him toss one down and I went over to pick it up. My Dad said very calmly, "That's hot." I picked it up anyway and it burned my hand so I dropped it. My Dad looked over his shoulder at me and smiled when he said "I told you it was hot." To which I replied, "no, it just doesn't take me long to look at a horseshoe." If you haven't been burned by the market let me give you some good advice, "That's hot." If you already know the danger and risk of the market then remember the "Kicking Mule Story."

I didn't use my common sense when I bought that first mutual fund. I had to be sold on the idea of mutual funds as it just didn't instinctively sit right with me. While the idea of higher future returns sounded appealing, losing the guarantee of growth made me nervous. Hearing in my head the phrase "past performance is no indication of future performance" made me feel like the investment was risky and the stock market was unpredictable.

And how many times will you invest in something that gives you the feeling of risk and unpredictability? Remembering what Pop had told me about the benefits of being able to figure out what your money will be worth in the future.

The second problem I had with mutual funds was what to do with the money in retirement. Building a nest egg and taking out the principal just didn't sit well with me, because it seems that the goal is to run out of life before you run out of money. That's just not a race I want to get into.

What I wanted, and what mutual funds didn't provide for me, was a way to be able to live off my interest payments. Not only did I want security that I would have money for the remainder of my life, but I wanted to be able to pass along the lump sum to my family.

In my pursuit of a safe way to incrementally grow my savings in a steady and profitable manner while being able to live off the interest and still pass the principal to my heirs, I stumbled upon an annuity salesman. He told me that if I put my money with him, I would have guaranteed payments for the rest of my life. However, I learned a tough lesson from my father on how annuities really worked.

My father spent most of his life working with General Motors, contributing to an annuity for 40 years, and through that time saved $70,000 for his retirement. When he turned 72, his principal 'annuitized' and he began receiving payments of $300 per month, and would continue receiving payments for the rest of his life. Unfortunately, he died 3 months later. Since his principal had annuitized, his beneficiaries were not able to receive the principal of $70,000, nor was my mother able to continue collecting the payments. My father spent forty years contributing to this plan to only receive a $900 return and have nothing left for his family.

To make matters worse, he died at the end of the month and the insurance company had the nerve to demand the last $300 check be returned.

Given the lessons taught to me by my Father and Grandfather, I chose not to put money in annuities or mutual funds. Rather, I wanted control of my financial future and I wanted to be able to combine the higher yields of mutual funds with the safety of a bank and the guaranteed payments of an annuity and still be able to pass my lifelong nest egg down to my family when I passed.

You see, I wanted to work like a bank, only better. Banks will take your money, invest it, keep all the collateral, and make 6-18% interest on this money. Then they turn around and pay you 0.5%. Doesn't seem fair, does it? Shouldn't you get the lion's share of the money?

What's done at Realbridge Solutions LLC is find people who have owner financed their house and would like to sell the note at a discount so they can get their money now. This plan not only allows you to accurately create a financial plan that will detail exactly what your money will be worth in the future, but it also provides you with a way to live off the payments, giving you something to pass down to your family.

▪ Invest In Gold

Man I hear it all the time on the radio and the TV. These days of uncertainty you need to buy gold. What they are telling you is your dollars are becoming worth less and less, where as their gold is becoming more and more valuable. It's time for a dose of "Common Sense" maybe even a double dose. So let me get this straight; they want you to send them your worthless money and because they think you are so special they will send you their precious gold. They obviously don't mind having all that worthless money and they want you to have the gold because gold has never been worth nothing. What do you think they are going to do with all that worthless money? Are they just waiting for gold to go back down so they can buy your worthless gold with their precious money?

What is the value of gold if the economy crashes? Do you think all the rich people will want jewelry? Wait a minute are the rich, rich because they have money or are they rich because they have gold?

I quoted Einstein before "the most powerful force in the universe is compound interest" he didn't say that appreciation was the most powerful force or interest was the most powerful force he said compound interest. How do you compound gold?

My common sense tells me that gold has very little value; you can't eat it and you can't live in it. You have to have faith that gold will do well in bad times. I remember in the early 70's gold was $800 dollar an ounce 40 years later its $1,500 an ounce—that's a whopping 1.57% annual growth rate. Remember religion requires faith; a sound financial plan requires a common sense application of information.

People buy gold because of the "conventional wisdom" they certainly don't buy it because of "common sense."

We have already talked about where I think you should invest your money now let's look at tax advantages.

▪ Defined Contribution Plan

Most of us are familiar with the defined contribution plan, such as a traditional 401k. You don't get much of a choice in a 401k. They are generally traditional in that you must pay taxes on all the money when you take it out. OUCH! The only choices you have in investments are all in the stock market.

IRA With a Broker

You get to pick whether you want a traditional IRA or a Roth but you can only buy from the broker's venders and only in the market. That's like the option people got when they got on the Titanic "do you want on the left side of the ship or the right side?"

Warning

I've seen the future and its 'ruff!' I'm sure you've seen the dramatic effect that Baby Boomers have on every market they enter. Look at school expansion when they reached school age and the car industry when they started driving. Look at home building when they grew up and got married and the explosion in the stock market when they started investing in their 401ks in the late 70's and early 80's. When the Baby Boomers enter or exit a market there is a quantum effect. There are 10,000 Baby boomers retiring every day now and that is what has Social Security on the ropes. In 2016 there is a huge calamity coming to the stock market call mandatory distribution from the IRAs.

The government delayed income taxes on money put into traditional IRAs until the money is withdrawn but they knew that some people would just leave their money in the IRAs so they would not have to pay the taxes. The IRS likes to collect taxes you've heard that old saying "pay me now or pay me later." The IRS has a rule that starting at age 70 and ½ if your money is in a traditional IRA you MUST start a mandatory distribution.

Think about that; 10,000 Baby Boomers a day start pulling their money out of the stock market and continue to do so until it's all out. Once it starts the market will continue to shrink. Even if you are not a Baby Boomer your 401k or IRA will be affected dramatically. The IRS can't afford to change the rules because they have already spent the increase in tax dollars this Boom Down will generate. I started this section with a Prince song let me end it with a Baby Boomer correct song from Bob Dylan "You better star swimming or you'll sink like a stone for the times they are a changing"

▪ Self-Directed IRA

If you have left the company where your 401k was you will want to roll the money over into a self-directed IRA.

A self-directed retirement plan is exactly what it says it is self-directed.

The person making the contributions is in complete control and has authority over what investments are placed into the plan.

- ☐ YOU choose the investment. (Mutual funds, gold, CDs, real estate notes, etc.)
- ☐ YOU structure the investment. (Tax qualified traditional IRA, Roth IRA or non-qualified.)
- ☐ YOU get to use common sense. (You can invest in almost anything except collectables or insurance.)

You can put your money in things that stock brokers, bankers and financial advisors don't earn a commission. So, if you ask advice from bankers, insurance agents, stockbrokers or financial planners remember this, "It's not that you can't do it; it's that they don't get paid when you do it."

Stuff about Self-Directed IRAs

Remember, these financial planners are all trained by Vendors. Vendors don't train their Representatives on how things work or on what all the options are; they train them how to sell their product.

They are getting paid a commission when they sell you their financial products (preferably the one with the highest commission), not when you pick the investment that benefits you the most. So of course, they'll object.

The point isn't that you shouldn't seek financial advice from them. In all fairness, some of them don't even know that you can self-direct your IRA. The firms that they work for have no interest in training them on self-directed retirement plans.

Remember that you always want to see the big picture and know all your options.

You might even hear that such a plan is illegal. But you now know better. One of the companies that will do a self-directed IRA for you is Sunwest Trust. They have a great web site that will give you needed information www.sunwesttrust.com.

Until recently, very few had heard about a self-directed IRA and using a retirement plan to buy real estate notes to earn income from what I think is one of the safest, most profitable investments in the history of business and finance.

The following are the two main types of self-directed IRA plans:

- ☐ The Traditional IRA: Created in 1974, the traditional IRA is a tax-deferred account in which contributions are made with pre-tax dollars subject to certain conditions pertaining to active participation in a qualified plan, provided certain contribution limits are not exceeded. This allows the money contributed to the traditional IRA to compound tax-free until funds are withdrawn. To qualify for a traditional IRA, an investor must be earning an income of any size and have not yet reached the age of 70 ½. The contribution limit for traditional IRAs was $5,000 in 2009 and 2010 ($6,000 if you're age 50 or older).

The main concern with the traditional IRA is that you are 'taxing the harvest rather than the seed.' For example, would you rather be taxed on a seed of corn or on the entire plant? Obviously paying taxes early on (seed) reduces your tax payment and ensures more money for you in the end. This philosophy is why many people enjoy the Roth IRA.

- ☐ The Roth IRA: Therefore, in 1997, Senator Roth of Delaware created an alternative to the Traditional IRA which allowed the owner to be taxed on the seed rather than the crop. The Roth IRA is a tax-free savings plan where the contributions are made with after-tax dollars, and therefore, are NOT tax deductible. All funds within the Roth IRA compound tax-free and all withdrawals from the account are also tax free (as long as the account owner is 59½ and the account has been opened for five years).

One of the main benefits of a Roth IRA is that there's no **required mandatory distribution** (RMD) at age 70½. Individuals can continue to contribute as long as they like, and all withdrawals continue to be tax free (if the account has been open for at least five years). Anyone who has earned income and falls within the MAGI (Modified Adjusted Gross Income) limits can establish a Roth IRA. The contribution limit for a Roth IRA was $5,000 in 2009 and 2011 ($6,000 if you're age 50 or older).

The ideal IRA would be one that is a self-directed, invested in something that pays a high fixed interest rate and is backed by collateral. Make sense doesn't it?

In recent years the stock market has frequently suffered, no that's not right, you have suffered. In the last 20 years the stock market has lost 45% of its value—twice. Every time the market does that, even if you don't pull your money out and it climbs back to where it was, you lost something much more valuable than money, you lost time.

Time is the major factor in compounding interest. Corporate scandals (Enron, World Com), downsizing, and outsourcing have affected the way many investors look at investing in certain companies. Today's savvy investors want more control over their portfolios.

Self-Directed IRAs

MAKING YOUR IRA A Self-Directed IRA: I spent almost 5 years as a securities broker before I had ever heard of self-directed IRAs. I had received a great deal of training from mutual fund vendors like Van Kampen, Smith Barney, Morgan Stanley and The Franklin Funds, but none had ever mentioned to me that people can put their money in anything other than mutual funds nor did they bother to tell me that people could control their own investments.

If you haven't created a self-directed retirement account yet, it's not too late to get started no matter how old you are; you'll find out it is pretty quick and easy to get started.

In the next few minutes you are going to learn something "New and Astonishing" that it will literally change you and your family's lives.

Once you learn these basic rules, you can make knowledgeable, confident decisions. There will be no more placing your family's entire financial future in the hands of so called experts who couldn't care less about them.

The reason you don't hear much about self-directed IRAs is simple is the people that put you in your IRA or 401(k) don't make any money from self-directed IRA.

IRS General Rules

The IRS regulations that govern IRAs allow you to put your money in anything other than life insurance or collectables (art, rare stamps, and foreign coins, etc.). Most of the money in IRAs and 401(k) s is in the stock market in mutual funds that you do not get to choose. The experts that do choose where your money goes just might not have your best interest at heart. You, on the other hand, always have your best interest at heart so you need to make some decisions. This explanation of how self-directed IRAs work is offered so the person with your best interest at heart will be in charge of your future, you.

A self-directed IRA works just like any IRA where you have a choice on how you want to save.

Traditional IRA and most 401ks: The money you put in the IRA is not taxed nor is the growth, but when you pull the money out it is all taxed as regular income.

Roth IRA: The money you put in is taxed but the growth is not. When you take the money out at age 59 1/2, regardless of how much it grew, there is no tax.

It is better to pay a small tax on the money you put in the program and no tax on all the growth when you retire than save a few dollars by paying income tax on all the growth when you retire. So you have two options; pay tax on the crop or pay tax on the seed.

It summarizes the primary laws which govern traditional IRAs.

What is a traditional Individual retirement account (traditional IRA)?

IRA stands for Individual Retirement Account so the is no such thing as a joint retirement account. I find the easiest way to visualize what an IRA is, is to think of it as a tax blanket that you can lay over your retirement investments, no matter what they are in, to either defer taxes or eliminate them. In other words, IRAs are not savings, they are simple a way to reduce taxes on savings.

A traditional IRA was the first tax-deferred savings account authorized by Internal Revenue Code section 408. It is a unique and simple way to encourage people to save money for retirement.

What are your tax benefits from a traditional IRA?

You may put in up to a certain amount of what you make, based on the year you contribute and your age, to your IRA account and have it be either fully or partially tax deductible (see deductibility chart). If your contribution is tax deductible, then you receive two tax benefits:

1) an immediate tax savings because you will pay fewer taxes because of the deduction, and
2) the earnings generated by the IRA funds are not taxed until distributed (deferred).

If your contribution is not tax deductible (because you make too much money to qualify), you still receive the tax benefit of tax deferral on the IRA's earnings. You may also qualify for a new tax credit.

The Contribution Rules

When do I have to establish the traditional IRA? You have until April 15, to establish and fund your IRA for the previous tax year. In other words if by April 14, 2012, you have not set up an IRA for 2011 you can still get it done.

The IRS is letting you play catch up if you are older you can put more money in. What are the contribution limits for a person who is not age 50 or older? For 2008-2011 - $5,000. What are the contribution limits for a person who is age 50 or older? For 2008-2011 - $6,000.

PUTTING TIDES TO WORK

To summarize, TIDES stands for reducing your **T**axes, reducing your out of pocket expense for your life **I**nsurance, paying off your **D**ebt, funding your **E**ssentials, and putting this freed up money into **S**avings for your retirement planning. So let's take a look at how this works.

Taxes - First, let's say you start a simple business. Let's say it's a multi-level marketing (MLM) company and you advertise and sell the product online. For the purpose of this example, we won't even consider any income that you will be generating; rather we'll focus on your deductions.

Having a business will allow you to write off some of your existing expenses, such as internet charges, phone bills, office supplies, etc... Also, you will be able to deduct your term life insurance and health insurance before paying your taxes. You now can go to your full time job and adjust your tax deductions to start collecting more money each month. For the purpose of this example, let's say that you are able to free up and apply $177 per month towards your debt.

Insurance - Next, you decide to get rid of your cash-value life insurance and buy term. This frees up and $90 a month for you to pay off debt with.

Debt - Now you have freed up a simple $267 per month that you can use to pay down your debt. The way we will allocate the funds is to put the first $200 into a self-directed IRA account that will grow you money (will discuss in the savings section) and use the remaining $67 to pay off debt.

You always want to start off paying the smallest debt first and then move on to the next smallest, simply because you will see results faster that way. Since the credit card debt is smallest, we'll pay off the smallest credit card debt first. Then we'll add the amount we were using to pay that small credit card to the $67 and use it to focus on paying off the next smallest credit card. Then we move to student loans and car loans. We continue this process until all debt is paid off.

In this example, there are 3 credit cards, a student loan, and a car loan to pay off, totaling $30,350 in debt.

If you use an extra $67 per month, you will pay off the first credit card in 13 months. Then you can use the extra $156.67 on top of the $95 already allocated to pay off the Chase credit card and contribute $251.67 a month.

This Chase card will then be paid off in full in 4 months. Roll the extra funds to the Bank of America card and he'll be contributing $461.67 per month to this account and have it paid off in two short months.

This process continues until we pay off all the debt. If you follow the process in the following example, the debt would be paid off within 26 months!

See the following diagram on how we've freed up that money, he has an extra $1,276 per month to put into paying off his house payment.

For example, assume you had a mortgage of $150,000 with a 6% interest rate, making the payments $899.33 per month. You have been paying 7 years on this mortgage already. If you were to "up" your payment by the amount of money you've already freed up, or an additional $1276, you will pay off your mortgage 7 years and 10 months!

CURRENT DEBT OVERVIEW	Owed	Monthly Payment
Visa	**$1,750**	**$90.00**
Chase	**$1,800**	**$95.00**
Bank of America	**$3,800**	**$210.00**
Student Loan	**$7,000**	**$392.00**
Car Loan	**$16,000**	**$489.00**
	$0	**$0.00**
	$0	**$0.00**
Totals	**$30,350**	**$1,276.00**

Total amount available per month to apply towards debt payoff:	**$66.67**

Owed	Monthly Payment
$1,750	$90.00
13 month	***$156.67***

Funds available to retire debt =	**$156.67**

Owed	Monthly Payment
$1,800	$95.00
4 months	***$251.67***

Funds available to retire debt =	**$251.67**

Owed	Monthly Payment
$3,800	$210.00
2 months	***$461.67***

Funds available to retire debt =	**$461.67**

Owed	Monthly Payment
$7,000	$392.00
0 months	***$853.67***

Funds available to retire debt =	**$853.67**

Owed	Monthly Payment
$16,000	$489.00
7 months	***$1,342.67***

Total number of payments to retire all debt:	**26**	months
Or	**2.17**	years

WAX ON-WAX OFF

If you've gotten this far, you are now a Black Belt in **Financial Common Sense.** Go to the link below watch a short video.

http://www.youtube.com/watch?v=Z4dkuYro4t8&feature=related

I think the moral of Wax on-Wax Off is: You can be enthusiastic about your future plans, but you should not start on the path of your plans with the preconceived ideas of conventional wisdom. You should first take some time off to notice your environment, surroundings and the elements around you. You should understand that there's a lesson in every element and these lessons are already hard-wired into your common sense. And most of all, you should understand that little things can build the path to success. You need to become more aware of the value and significance of details and understand that little and seemingly insignificant things are the bricks that build the wall of success, for there's a lesson in every step.

Poncho Villa was playing with some of his friends one day and they decided to have a contest to see who could draw the straightest line in the dirt with a stick between where they were standing and a large Oak tree. Each boy took his turn drawing a foot or two then backing up and studying their wavy line. When it became Poncho's turn he won the contest by walking straight to the tree dragging the stick behind him. Keep what you want in front of you and walk straight to it.

So let's go through the Wax on-Wax Off drill. You now know that the only way you are ever going to be able to retire in the manner you want is if you are able to find the money to put aside. You also know all the well keep secretes; you know **WHERE** to find the money. You know **WHERE** to put the money. You know **WHAT** you have to do and **WHEN** you need to do it. Just in case you didn't really read the book and just skipped to the end, let me go over those again.

(**WHERE**) You know you can find the money to pay off all your debt, live a better life and retire the way you want by using the Financial Blueprint to guide you through the TIDES System. (**WHERE**) You realize that the best place to put the money is where you are paid a fixed interest rate and have collateral.

(WHAT) You have to get a free Financial Blueprint because that is the only way to get a customized plan. **(WHEN)** There is a law; "The Law of Diminishing Intent!" which means it's easy to change your destiny by taking action now but unfortunately, it easy not to. The longer you wait the easier it will be to accept an average life. The great philosopher Jim Rohn said "If you don't know where to start, simply throw a rock in the air, where ever it lands start there." Too many people spend their lives asking an unanswerable question—why? The right question would change everything in their and their family's future—the question should be **when**? Because the answer is **NOW! DO IT NOW!!!**

Is It Too Late Even If You Are Already Broke?

> There is a tide in the affairs of men,
> Which, taken at the flood, leads on to fortune;
> Omitted, all the voyage of their life
> Is bound in shallows, and in miseries.
> On such a full sea are we now afloat;
> And we must take the current when it serves,
> Or lose our ventures.
>
> Brutus. Julius Caesar Act IV Scene 3: Within the Tent of Brutus.

If I could show you the way out of your present financial mess where you would feel better about yourself and your future, would you like to see it? Can you imagine what it would be like to go through December without that knot in your stomach because you don't know how you can pay for it? That is exactly what I promise I can do.

You are probably your own worst enemy. You are beating yourself up worse than anybody. If you can look yourself in the eye and answer this question honestly, with what your real aim was when you got in this mess, there is nothing that can stop you from kicking down the door to your future success. I never met you, but I know you. I have walked a mile in your shoes. If you were not a GOOD PERSON you would not be reading this book; you really wouldn't care.

Right now you have probably exhausted every idea trying to avoid what is about to happen to you and doubtless to your family. You go to bed every night and wake up every day stressing about it. You're only a bad person *if* when you made you mark on that contract for all your debt you knew you would not pay it back. So here's the question, was it your plan to pay it back? If you honestly answered "yes" then stop playing the "if I had only" game and start your journey toward the bright side of the road.

You are a good person, you are a good person, and you are a good person. You give to other people when they need help, you get mad at injustice, and you are never cruel on purpose. If you intended to pay it back and the circumstance changed or you miscalculated, then it was a mistake. It was not your fault nor was it anybody else's fault—it just happened.

There is nothing more evil than evil intent. You had no evil intent. I know that sounds very simplistic. Your critic will criticizes you and say you should have known better. They can play Monday morning quarterback because they have the luxury of hindsight. You bought into the conventional wisdom of the times and the conventional wisdom was charged and charged because everything would keep getting better and better. Now you can see that you previous course is no longer the way to go. Once you have reached the point of no return and you recognize it, you should simply get off the dead horse; take your saddle bags with and as much of your stuff as you can carry and walk away.

Don't pour the rest of your water in the dead horse's mouth; you will most assuredly need it to survive. The only thing you should bear in your mind is the lesson you learned—no guilt, no blame just the lesson. You need to start planning the rest of your life for not only yourself but your family. In the movie X Caliber if the King was sick, the kingdom was sick. You owe everyone that loves you a better life. You can't succeed if your mistake is always in front of you, put it in the past and move on. Get thee behind me, Satan.

Let's talk about your critics; you know who they will be. I can see you waking up at 3:30 in the morning stressing about what "they" will say and think about you and what story you will tell them. This happened to me so many times I named it "The Dragon's Breath." First things first, what other people think of you is none of your business. It doesn't matter if someone you know has gone broke and spent 10 years of their life paying back every stinking penny they owed. That person may have fed his own ego with the sacrifice he made so he could brag about how he suffered, how he paid them every penny, how he is proud of himself. Heartaches are heroes when your pockets are full. He is proud because he is a man of his word, but how much did his family pay so he would feel better about himself?

Shakespeare said, "To thine own self be true." You already answered the question about did you mean to cheat anyone. You need to start looking at this from the stand point that this was a mistake you made and you will get through it. To you it was personal, but to everybody else it was business. Thank God this is America and going broke is not a crime. I hope you realize that **GOING BROKE IS NOT A CRIME**. In your life you make a lot of promises, some more important than others like I promise I will take the trash out in the morning or I promise you, son, that if you get good grades, I will pay for your college. Anyone can pick the big promise out of those two choices.

There isn't any more important promise than one you make your family. If you need to make a decision between your family's well-being and the warm fuzzy feeling you get by paying all your Visa bills; make sure you make the right one. Do you want it written on you tombstone "Here lies a loving father who always put his family first" or "Here lies a man who paid back every stinking penny he owed." Not making a decision is making the wrong decision.

I believe that the pride many people have in paying back every debt they owe is more to stroke their own egos. Keeping the promises they made their family is number one. The late, great financial philosopher Jim Rohn asked a grade school class what the meaning of the word "Resolve" was. He got a lot of answers but a young pig-tailed girl raised her hand and gave the best answer he had ever heard, she said "Resolve is a promise you make yourself."

You need to resolve to take care of your family first and Visa second. My definition of a fool is someone who lies to themselves and believes it. Scarlett at the climax of "Gone With the Wind" resolved "I'm never going to be hungry again." At the end of this chapter of your life make your resolve.

I believe that Mohammed Ali was the greatest Heavy Weight Champion of all time, not because he was never beaten, he lost almost 10% of his fights (56-5), but I think he was the greatest because he always believed he was "The Greatest" even when he lost, he always believed he would win the next time because he learned something. He always got up and came back. The Barron von Richthofen crashed 3 times before he learned how to fly. George Washington lost more battles than he won. Abraham Lincoln failed in business and politics many times before he succeeded. Failure is essential for success. Most of the financial experts have a bunch of vendor-trained knowledge but few have experienced what you are going through right now; I have.

I wrote a blog "If You Can't Pay Your Bills, Don't Pay Your Bills," which I have included and begins on page 94. You would think I killed a puppy by the way the financial experts attacked me. One wrote that everything I wrote was "Garbage" and that I had "no ethic" for telling people that if they could not pay their bills to not pay their bills. He went on to prove to me how much better he was than any of you unethical people who, because you can't pay your bills, should pay your bills. He bragged that he had gone broke and it took him 6 years to pay back every single penny he owed. I wrote him back and ask him if he believed that people who **couldn't** pay their bills, then they should pay their bills? (The logic of this escaped my common sense.) I did this because I thought he was a "moron" but I wanted to be sure. Pray tell how you are supposed to pay your bills if you don't have enough money to pay your bills. I guess if you don't pay your bill because you don't have enough money you should flog yourself with a stick and that is exactly what some of you do.

Because I understand you, I know you would give almost anything to just pay back all of your creditors, if you could. Most of this book is about how to do just that, but I seem to be the only writer who realizes that in America a lot of people are already passed the point of being able to do that. The first 11 chapters of this book deals with how to pay off all of your debt, after you get out of your current financial mess you too can apply these methods. But for you to get out of this mess and move forward—you have to get over your guilt.

You have to keep faith in yourself; you did not plan on any of this to happen. The only thing that would help is more money and I'm sure you have already exhausted that avenue. Did you ever go swimming with your friends when you were young and one of them held your head underwater? How bad did you want that next breath? That's probably the same want you have now for some money. You're feeling bad does not help; it hurts.

▪ Be Careful What You Give Your Life To

IF YOU CAN'T PAY YOUR BILLS, DON'T PAY YOUR BILLS

If you look back at history, we Americans have always looked up to people who were proactive; people who were in a bad circumstance and did whatever it took to change those circumstances. For instance, the Pilgrims were persecuted for their religion. At some point they decided "We can either stay here in England and be persecuted or we can pack up and go to America." We admire their ability to take control of a situation.

The history of the world is full of stories where people had to make a decision either to continue to suffer or brave the unknown and chose freedom from your share-cropper contracts. I'm sure there were people who called them quitters. People who told them just conform to the "Conventional Wisdom" and everything will be just fine.

Why the history lesson in a financial blog? What could persecution have to do with debt? I believe that DEBT COLLECTION is a form of persecution that has become so ingrained in our society that we don't even recognize it. We accept the authority and moral guidance from people and institutions that, in truth, have no authority and surely have no morals and the only guidance they have is the Judas kind. We have all heard of people who have had heart attacks after dealing with these credit collectors.

Did you vote or did you have your Congressman set up an agency that can collect information on you in secret and sell it to the highest bidder? Did you think it would just be great if this agency set up a "Double Secret scoring formula that is guarded better than the formula for Coke, which can dictate how much money almost everything cost you, where you live, what you drive, where your kids go to school and even how much your car insurance cost?" Oh I know you thought, "Wouldn't it be fun if every time you violated any of this wonderful agency's rule they could maybe call you at work and home and harass you, make you feel like a real deadbeat because you missed one of their payments?" If you didn't give the credit bureaus this power, then they really don't have it.

I have been doing radio shows all over America for the last few years. Many times I have had people come up and thank me for simplifying the complicated mess that they were in. A lady caller told me she had worked all of her life at the same place. She had raised 2 kids by herself. The owner of her company was killed in a car accident and the business was closed. She had bought a new house the year before. While looking for a new job she spent all her IRA money and charge up her credit cards paying one with another. The mortgage market bottomed out and she owed about $50,000 more than her house was worth. She had taken another job at half her pay just to buy food and gas but she was getting farther and farther behind on her mortgage, credit cards and car payments. She could keep trying to keep it together. She could work out deals with her creditors that she knew she couldn't keep and she was going to lose it all anyway. She could pour the last of her water in the dead horse's mouth, but it would not improve her credit or her family's future.

She talked to a bankruptcy attorney but she didn't even have the money to pay him and even if she did, bankruptcy would not solve her problem. That house payment was killing her. In fact the way she sounded, I would say pressure was getting to be too much for her to bear. She had to stop talking twice because she was crying. I was having a hard time not crying with her. Conventional wisdom would not get her out of this mess. No matter how strong her desire to pay back the money she owed, she could not. It was tearing her up inside. Do you think those two sweet little girls were wondering "what wrong with Mommy?"

I could tell this was a good-hearted lady that had come to the end and needed some relief. She would always answer the phone calls from her creditor and try to explain her problem. They showed no mercy and berated her and made her feel like a crook. Her Aunt told her to call my radio show "Warr On Debt" that she had heard me tell other good people that had "Mortgage Cancer" the cure.

Here is what I said. The first thing you need to do is stop the phone calls from the Pustules (collection agents). Their sole purpose is to make her feel so bad about herself that she would pay them some money. They are very good at their job of collecting money by making people feel bad. I asked her if she had a cell phone; she said she did, so I told her to disconnect her home phone. I told her to call her friends and tell them that she did not need a home phone anymore.

Next stop paying any credit card companies anything. Stop paying any mortgage payments. Just those things would save her $1,700 per month. Her house payment was $900 per month, so I told her to save $400 per month in a tin can and bury in her back yard. It will take the mortgage company probably 8 or 12 months to make her move out her so when they do she will have close to $4,000 saved in her tin can. With $4,000 she can find another place to live painlessly. She was worried about not paying a debt she owes, so I told her that when her economic situation gets better to send whatever she thought was the right amount to the creditors with a money order that does not have her name on it. That way she feels better about paying her debt and they can't start up with her again because they don't know where the money came from.

I told her that not only is it possible to have a life with a low credit score but you can have a much more rewarding stress free life with a low credit score. You can still buy houses and cars and have credit cards but you will lower your use of them because you will have what a friend of mine calls "Warm Fluffy Cash." Cash is King.

The last thing I told her was that when you fly, before you take off the airline attendant always says, "If the oxygen mask drops put it on yourself first before you put it on your child." That because if you don't survive your child probably won't either. You are going to lose your house anyway. Make sure you have enough money to move, your credit is already shot for the next 7 years and bankruptcy stays on your record for 10 years. (She lived in Texas so they can't garnish her wage, but even if they did, it would be less than paying all the bills plus they don't know where she works or lives.) With bankruptcy you may still have to pay your credit cards and it ruins your credit anyway so why not keep the money now when you need it to have it to survive.

The businesses that lent you the money made a business decision that if you paid it all back they would make a lot of money. For instance If she would have keep the $150,000 house for 30 years at 6% with a payment of $900 she would have paid $324,000 for the house. That's $150,000 for the house and $174,000 for the interest. Now it's time for some more of that common sense math. Divide the principal into the interest to see what her real interest was. $174,000 divided by $150,000 = $1.16. For every dollar she would pay them in principal she would pay them $1.16 in interest. That is 116% interest not 6%. Frankly, knowing how they screwed you might help ease your mind; they wouldn't spit on you if you were on fire. They are a business; don't pretend they have a soul. Keep your word and pay them when you can, but you set the time table.

I told you that the financial experts would want to burn me at the stake but you cannot give your life to creditors; you need to live your life in a way that is good for you and your family. Your family needs to come first, even if it hurts your pride that you can't pay your bills. Art Williams wrote a book that the title tells the story. The title is "All You Can Do Is All You Can Do but All You Can Do Is Enough." Jesus said, "Go forth and sin no more." Start now! I always ended my show with this statement which I believe I follow "If I can help, I will" so if you would like my help email me at jw@JWAcademy.com.

Once we get you on the road to financial recovery you can decide how much to repay your creditor, and we will help you find the money. At that point you have no hope of getting a good credit score. That fact alone will make you have a better life so don't even worry about it. The Alcoholics Anonymous (AA) has a prayer they call the Serenity Prayer:

God, grant me the serenity to accept the things I cannot change, the courage to change the things I can, and the wisdom to know the difference.

To get a second chance to start over from 0 is a way to accelerate your recovery. A doctor called me the other day that really had no way out. I told him that when he finally comes to the realization that the horse is dead—get off. Kicking a dead horse is an act of frustration, but trying to ride a dead horse is stupid. I ask him if he had ever had way too much to drink and felt like he needed to throw up but keep on fighting it and fighting it till finally he threw up. I asked, "How did you feel after you threw up?" His answer was, "Better." You will feel so much better after you make a decision.

You will still be able to buy a car; you will probably have cash, but if not, the interest rate will be high. You should just rent or lease a house because renters spend about 26% less on lodging than owners. You really have to think of having bad credit for a while as a game. Because you have bad credit you will have more money than the people with good credit.

If you can't buy on credit you become less of an impulse buyer. Since you are not an impulse buyer you have to save your money to buy things. Since you pay cash for things they cost you less. It's like you are in an exclusive buying club where you get a big discount on everything you buy. Now you have a secret.

When my daughter Julie was little, my wife and I took her to see a doctor because of her misaligned feet. He said that she would need to wear some special shoes with a bar between them while she slept. The doctor told us that Julie would either love or hate the shoes according to our attitude. So we made the "Night Night Shoes" a fun thing. It worked; when Julie didn't need the shoes any more she still wanted to wear them. Coming back from broke can be a fun game, a fun game you will win.

ABOUT THE AUTHOR

JW Warr has endured decades of "ups and downs" associated with building and owning businesses, the trauma of bankruptcy, and built insurance, securities and owner-financed mortgages businesses from scratch. Because he didn't clutter his thoughts with formal schooling, he developed a sharp mind, without preconceived notions, able to view finances in a fresh way. JW is only happy when he can take something that on the surface looks very complicated and makes it simple...In fact "Simple" is his favorite word.

www.JWAcademy.com

Made in the USA
Charleston, SC
24 June 2012